D0622478

Christianity and the Culture of Economics

Religion, Culture and Society

Series Editors:
Oliver Davies,
Department of Theology and Religious Studies,
University of Wales, Lampeter
and Gavin Flood,
Department of Religious Studies,
University of Stirling

Religion, Culture and Society is a series presented by leading scholars on a wide range of contemporary religious issues. The emphasis throughout is generally multicultural, and the approach is often interdisciplinary. The clarity and accessibility of the series, as well as its authoritative scholarship, will recommend it to students and a non-specialist readership alike.

Christianity and the Culture of Economics

Edited by

DONALD A. HAY
and
ALAN KREIDER

UNIVERSITY OF WALES PRESS
CARDIFF
2001

British Library Cataloguing-in-Publication Data
A catalogue record for this book is available from the British Library.

ISBN 0-7083-1704-9 (paperback)
0-7083-1711-1 (hardback)

Website: www.wales.ac.uk/press

Typeset by Mark Heslington, Scarborough, North Yorkshire
Printed in Great Britain by Dinefwr Press, Llandybïe

Contents

List of figures

List of tables

List of Figures

List of Tables

Preface

This collection of essays forms the third volume published by the University of Wales Press in association with the Centre for the Study of Christianity and Culture at Regent's Park College, Oxford.

The Centre for the Study of Christianity and Culture fosters study into a wide range of topics in the area of Christianity and culture, and works in close co-operation with the Principal and Fellows of Regent's Park College in a range of theological and interdisciplinary studies. This is reflected in the publication so far of volumes entitled *Culture and the Nonconformist Tradition*, *The Novel, Spirituality and Modern Culture*, and now *Christianity and the Culture of Economics*. All began life as public lectures given in the Centre at Regent's Park College.

It will be evident that the Centre is engaging with a wide range of contemporary cultural issues from a Christian perspective, but none is more significant and pressing than this volume on 'Christianity and the culture of economics'. It brings together a distinguished group of contributors, with wide-ranging experience and expertise, to offer insights from government, legal, academic and voluntary sectors. Together they make a significant and unique contribution to the wider discussion on the forces of 'global capitalism' and the ethics of the market-place.

I am grateful to the editors, Professor Donald A. Hay, Head of the Social Science Division in the University of Oxford, and Dr Alan Kreider, my predecessor as the Director of the Centre for the Study of Christianity and Culture, for their work in arranging the original series of lectures (given in Michaelmas Term 1999) and in preparing this volume for publication; and to the

University of Wales Press for publishing it as part of the Press's Religion, Culture and Society series.

Nicholas J. Wood
Oxford
Trinity Term, 2001

Centre for the Study of Christianity and Culture
Regent's Park College
Oxford

The Contributors

Isabella D. Bunn is a Fellow of the Centre for the Study of Christianity and Culture, Regent's Park College, Oxford.

Andrew Dilnot is Director of the Institute of Fiscal Studies, London.

Bob Goudzwaard is Professor of Economics at the Free University, Amsterdam.

Lord Griffiths of Fforestfach is International Adviser, Goldman Sachs International.

Donald A. Hay is Head of the Division of Social Sciences, University of Oxford, and Professorial Fellow of Jesus College, Oxford.

Andrew Henley is Professor of Economics and Head of Economics Group, School of Management and Business, University of Wales, Aberystwyth.

Donald B. Kraybill is Professor of Sociology and Anabaptist Studies at Messiah College, Grantham, Pennsylvania.

Alan Kreider is former Director of the Centre of the Study of Christianity and Culture, Regent's Park College, Oxford, and now Adjunct Faculty in Church History, Associated Mennonite Biblical Seminary, Elkhart, Indiana.

David Nussbaum is Finance Director, Oxfam.

Roger Sawtell is a founder of the Daily Bread Co-operative, Northampton.

1

Introduction: the role of values in a market economy

DONALD A. HAY

The issue addressed in this volume of essays is the origin and role of values in a market economy. There are two views of this matter, and the essays can be understood as an extended discussion of these two views. The first view is that the market is no more than a mechanism for allocating resources, and that the allocations that result reflect values that are brought to markets by participants. So consumers make decisions about what they will buy, and how much they will work and save. Firms make their decisions responding to 'consumer sovereignty' over what goods should be produced. If consumers demand 'good' goods then those will be supplied: if they demand trash, then trash will be provided. The most successful firms will be those that meet the market test of relevance to consumer needs. Equally firms have to motivate their workers to supply labour, and to work productively at work. A successful firm, therefore, will be one that matches its job characteristics to the hours and types of work that potential workers are willing to supply. If potential workers have materialistic values seeking high levels of personal consumption, then they will want to work long hours to maximize incomes, and will not care too much about keeping work within bounds so as to have more time for family life or community involvement. If, on the other hand, potential workers have preferences for time out of work rather than consumption, then those preferences will also be accommodated by employers. Indeed one of the perceived advantages of the market mechanism is that it can accommodate more than one set of preferences at any one time. Some firms can produce 'good' goods and services, while others produce trash. Some working contracts can emphasize high material rewards for long working hours; others can provide much lower returns for those who prefer to consume less and have more time for family and friends.

The second view is that, far from being a neutral mechanism, the market develops its own internal values. In particular, the accusation is that the market is at the very least conducive to, and at worst active in promoting, selfish and materialistic behaviour. This accusation is summarized clearly in the essay by Griffiths, who cites both secular and Christian critics of the market economy. The substance of the accusation is that in practice the promotion of the market in the UK has resulted in a culture of greed, hedonism and materialism, based in a new and strident individualism, and in a loss of any concern for the common good and in particular for the poor. Secular critics lament the loss of wider cultural values and institutions; Christian critics underline the departure from Christian moral standards. Not least there has been a narrowing of ethical perspectives: economic 'rationality' is invading domains of human flourishing and activity, which previously were conducted on entirely different criteria – marriage and the family are critical examples. Marriage becomes a contract rather than a covenant, and the relationships between parents and children are viewed as trading across time of reciprocated services rather than as expressions of human love.

How might we resolve this contrast of views on the market? The essays explore the question along a number of different routes. The first viewpoint is that of those who have been actively involved in the day-to-day operations and management of business and finance in the UK (Griffiths, Nussbaum). A second viewpoint is that of those who have engaged in market activities, but have brought to their businesses a very different set of values from those of most market participants (Kraybill, Sawtell). A third perspective comes from the design and implementation of economic policies which explicitly introduce some apparently 'non-market' values into the operations of a variety of different markets (Bunn, Henley, Dilnot). A final perspective comes from academic economists and concerns the values implicit in the economic analysis which is used to explicate and evaluate economic behaviour in markets (Goudzwaard, Hay). I introduce these contributions in turn here with a view to providing some signposts for the reader before he or she tackles the content of each of the essays.

The contrast between the contributions of Lord Griffiths and David Nussbaum is quite striking. Lord Griffiths of Fforestfach (then Brian Griffiths) was a distinguished academic economist who became head of the policy unit at 10 Downing Street during the period when Margaret Thatcher was prime minister. It is evident that he played a considerable part in the 'Thatcher revolution', with its emphases on liberalizing markets, and on privatization. He left Downing Street when Margaret Thatcher lost the support of the Conservative Party, and began a new career as an international investment banker, working for Goldman Sachs. David Nussbaum had a successful business career as finance director of a listed company, before leaving to join Oxfam as head of finance. Both reflect on their experience of working in a market environment. Lord Griffiths's position is that the market reflects the values of those who work in it and does not promote values of its own. So he affirms 'I . . . do not believe the market system *per se* has a bias to materialism'. On the contrary he reports that his experience in the City of London and as a non-executive director of more than ten companies in both the UK and the USA is very different from the criticisms of those who look at the market from the outside. He notes that there is in fact a great deal of highly responsible and ethically motivated behaviour. This leads him to develop his thesis that a case for the market can be constructed on the basis of a theology of wealth creation. Five theological themes are explored: human creativity as a reflection of our nature in the image of God, human rationality reflecting our God-given capacity to make choices for good and evil, the need for community arising from a Trinitarian understanding of God in whose image we are made, concern for the poor and disadvantaged and the need to give them opportunities to develop their potential, and the obligation to serve implied in the injunction to serve our neighbours. Griffiths's argument is that all these theological desiderata are met by a market economy: indeed he goes further to claim that the market economy should be accorded the same priority for human flourishing as the family and the political authorities. His conclusion is that the market gives excellent opportunities for ethically motivated people to pursue good behaviour rather than bad, and that we should not despair of introducing norms that are closer to Christian or humanistic values. There is no justification for allowing other, less attractive, values and behaviour to dominate.

David Nussbaum starts from the perception of the aims of business as reflected in the finance and management literature on 'shareholder value'. This does not hesitate to affirm that the primary aim of a company is to maximize the value of the company to the shareholders, in contrast to the view that a company has a responsibility to a variety of stakeholders including customers, workers, the community and the environment. Nussbaum documents this view in a range of influential literature including the views of business academics, consultants and accountants. The incentives for the management of businesses to adopt this primary aim are threefold. First, there are the sticks: a firm that does not maximize shareholder value will probably be a target for shareholder activism, and possibly will be the target of a hostile takeover in which the senior management are certain to lose their jobs. Second, there are the carrots: executives are increasingly offered incentive payments linked in some way to the performance of the share price of the firm. Third, there is accountability: maximizing shareholder value is an unambiguous objective in comparison with the multiple values that have to be juggled under a stakeholder model. Running a business is complex, and setting multiple objectives would make it impossible. While there is nothing in Nussbaum's discussion to demonstrate that maximization of shareholder value has to be the sole objective of business, it is apparent that there is a huge gulf between his view of the reality of business life and the more benign version of business behaviour in a market economy presented by Griffiths.

The second line of enquiry into the values of the market economy is to look at case-studies of businesses that have operated in a secular market economy but with very different values. The chapter by Roger Sawtell tells the story of employee-owned co-operatives in the UK, with a particular emphasis on the Industrial Common Ownership Movement, which was founded in 1971, and on the Daily Bread Co-operative of which Sawtell was a founder member. By 1996 there were over 1,000 co-operative businesses in the UK, the majority of which were very small, but with some larger firms such as the John Lewis Partnership and Scott Bader. The strongly counter-cultural characteristics of some of these enterprises is illustrated by the description of the Daily Bread Co-operative. The working members are all Christians, and there is a daily half-hour meeting for worship, Bible study and prayer. There is a weekly meeting to make decisions about the business, but between meetings the manager has the authority to implement decisions as he or she sees best. Salaries are modest, and the same for all workers regardless of their responsibilities within the business, but additional allowances are paid to those with dependants to care for. The business regularly provides employment for those recovering from mental illness, seeking to give them support while they re-establish themselves in society. The modest surpluses generated by the business are donated to Third World charities. The interesting fact is that common-ownership businesses like Daily Bread have enjoyed modest economic success over the last twenty-five years: a lower proportion have failed than in businesses in general, and they have grown without becoming indebted. The conclusion is that businesses that are run on other than shareholder-value-maximizing lines can survive and indeed thrive in the secular market-place. Since 1996 the legal framework has made it easier to set up a worker-owned business, and Sawtell predicts that common ownership is an idea whose time has come at last.

A very different counter-culture is described in the chapter by Donald Kraybill on the involvement of Amish people in small businesses in the United States. The Amish, a flourishing tradition emerging from the Anabaptist movement of the Reformation era, have developed a culture many of whose features run contrary to the prevailing social paradigms. Three are of particular significance. The first is the priority given to collective wisdom, mediated through the church, over individual choices. The second is the limitation of consumption by individual families, and especially the avoidance of ostentation. The third is the rejection of modern technology, including electricity from the mains, automobiles and trucks, telephones and computers. Originally these cultural features were maintained in a context of a purely agrarian economy, but from the late 1970s the Amish have increasingly been involved in microenterprises. The reason for this is largely demographic: the Amish have large families, and for the most part the children grow up and remain in the local church communities. Shortage of land made it imperative that alternative economic activities be developed. Kraybill shows that they have been very successful in developing microenterprises in crafts and manufactured products, despite the apparent handicaps imposed by their culture. In some communities he surveyed, over 50 per cent of adults were so employed. The question is the extent to which their involvement in non-Amish markets has compromised their culture. The answer seems to be: not much – yet. Various devices have been found for taking on necessary technologies without direct compromise; for example, the use of hydraulic power instead of electricity to drive machine tools, and the buying in of services such as transport and computing that the Amish deny themselves. Once again the evidence is consistent with the position advanced by Brian Griffiths that a market economy can accommodate even quite extreme deviance from general cultural norms on the part of some participants in markets. But it is also apparent that keeping cultural defences in place is a difficult task, and requires extreme vigilance on the part of the community.

The third route to address the values of the market focuses on public policy. The question is whether additional values other than those existing in the market can be successfully introduced by appropriate public policies. Thus, Isabella Bunn, who specializes in international law, provides an analysis of attempts to introduce values into the activities of the World Trade Organization. She lists five areas where it has been argued (sometimes successfully) that considerations other than the promotion of trade should motivate decisions by the WTO. The first is 'protection of public morals', and this has been invoked in circumstances ranging from the ban on importation of non-kosher meat into Israel to the prevention of trade in pornographic material. The second is assistance to developing economies, which have been accorded some exceptions from a rigorous free-trade regime: the question of the access of such economies to technologies has also been raised with the suggestion that the protection of at least some patents should be weakened. The third area is concern for the environment, and the frequent suggestions that trade in products that are produced in ways that are directly or indirectly detrimental to the global or local environment should be banned. A fourth area is labour standards: the argument is that products that are produced without a concern for the welfare of workers should be banned. The particularly emotive examples involve the use of child labour in some Third World countries. Finally, there has been the concern of Western policy-makers to make access to world markets under the WTO dependent on human rights. The sanctions imposed on South Africa in the apartheid era are the best-known example. Bunn questions how far the use of trade law is effective in pursuing these objectives. She notes that there is a wide diversity of cultural norms among the nations involved in world trade, and it is unclear whose consciences should prevail in deciding on trade policies relating to these issues. Moreover, the pursuit of other objectives presumes an institutional competence that the WTO lacks. Sanctions do not always have the desired effects, and may in any case impact most on innocent individuals rather than on the political authorities who are responsible for the violations of ethical principles in their domestic affairs. It is possible that trade does more to change attitudes as it promotes shared values internationally.

Andrew Henley, who is an academic economist with specialist interests in labour markets, addresses issues with respect to work and employment. His starting-point is a set of biblical perspectives on work, which he uses to critique the current situation. He notes that the biblical concept of stewardship sits uneasily with the dominant conception of work as a 'disutility' to be tolerated in order to be able to consume. The idea that work is intrinsic even to fallen human nature, and that it gives purpose and enrichment to life, is something other. Similarly the biblical conception of stewardship suggests a shared endeavour rather than individual workers working solely for themselves. Henley's concern is that by using a narrow model of human purposes in our analysis we fail to consider different ways in which work might be organized, with adverse consequences for the world of work. In a similar vein he questions the fashionable concern with labour-market flexibility. While this may have benefits in terms of employment and productivity, it can also have costs. Excessive mobility can lead to problems for family and community life, as workers move from job to job in different regions without putting down roots in a community. Similarly, the lack of job security within firms leads to lack of commitment and loss of a sense of joint endeavour among a group of workers. Finally, he draws attention to the problem of discrimination in the labour market. The key to escaping from unemployment or unskilled employment is often education and training. Providing the means for workers to escape is consistent with the Jubilee concept of providing for economic restoration and redemption, and a natural extension of the concept is to enable the disadvantaged to develop their human capital.

The third case-study is provided by Andrew Dilnot, who is the Director of the Institute for Fiscal Studies and an expert on social security in the UK. His starting-point is that 'the provision of welfare is inevitably bound up with ethical judgements, so we should expect to be able to bring Christian faith to bear on this subject'. He details the tension implicit in the current state of welfare. First, expenditure on welfare (health, education and social security) has grown hugely since the inception of the welfare state in the 1940s, and there are pressures for continued growth. Second, the welfare state in practice substantially redistributes income from the better off to the worse off, and that effect becomes more marked as the underlying distribution of income becomes more unequal. Third, there is a perceived unwillingness of taxpayers to accept increases in their taxes, and indeed political parties are highly sensitive to charges that their expenditure plans will require higher taxes. Governments have dealt with this tension by various means, of which the most significant are the pronounced shift to means-tested benefits in place of universal benefits, and the encouraging of self-reliance (for example, private pensions) and work (for example, programmes designed to get people into work). However, these may make the tension worse, as the welfare state focuses a greater share of expenditure on the poorest groups in place of 'universal' provision, thus making the redistributive effect even stronger and increasing the probability that taxpayers will be unwilling to foot the bill. Over and against this tension there remains a public commitment to maintaining the welfare state which is based on a very strong ethical sense that the most vulnerable groups in society should be protected and cared for. The question is whether this commitment and ethical stance can be sustained in the face of the market values that have put down such strong roots in British culture in the last twenty years. Andrew Dilnot identifies some of the key non-market values that Christians might wish to be upheld: that people should be valued for what they are, and not only for what they contribute economically; that our incomes are not, as the property rights view asserts, ours by rights but by gift; and that financial self-interest is not the only, or even the best, motivation for our market behaviour. Such non-market values are essential to underpin the concept of the welfare state, and to guide in the formation of specific policies.

A fourth route to evaluating the values of the market system is to examine the role of ethical values within the discipline of economics, both as a theoretical social science and as applied to questions of economic and social policy. This question is explored in the chapters by Bob Goudzwaard and myself. Professor Goudzwaard has had a distinguished career both as a practising economist and in the public policy arena in Holland, and has written a number of influential books arguing for a reconsideration of the fundamental bases of both economic analysis and economic policy. In his chapter he contrasts the concerns of modern economic analysis with outcomes measured in terms of economic growth and income per capita, with the emphases of the Old Testament economy for the right treatment of the inputs to the productive process, especially land and labour. Thus the worker is to be treated justly according to his needs, the land is to enjoy sabbatical rests to recover from cropping and the excessive accumulation of capital in a few hands is to be discouraged. Goudzwaard acknowledges that such an economy will be less productive than a modern market economy. But he notes that the latter is characterized by the exploitation of human beings, the destruction of the environment and the unequal distribution of capital across communities and nations, and asks whether the greater productivity is not being achieved at too great a cost in terms of human flourishing and environmental degradation. He admits that it will not be easy to broaden economic analysis and the policy agenda to incorporate concerns for inputs as well as outputs, since the established paradigm is so firmly entrenched. But his is a prophetic call for the rich economies of the West to wake up to the perils they face if they do not mend their profligate ways.

In my chapter I address three issues that face the practising economist who is also a Christian. The first is unease with the dominant values of mainstream economic analysis, which makes the fundamental assumption that all human behaviour is driven by self-interested economic rationality. This understanding of human behaviour is applied to every area of life, not just the distinctively economic. Family life, sexual relations, political processes are all to be viewed through this same methodological lens. There is no explicit normative content in this approach, but the implicit assumption that individuals are always the best judges of their own interests. So the objective of policy is to maximize the domain over which the individual can make choices. The methodology thus legitimizes self-seeking behaviour in every area of human life. The Christian response is to note that, while this model of human behaviour may not be inconsistent with the actual behaviour of fallen human beings, it is by no means an accurate description of what human beings made in the image of God should aspire to. How is the Christian economist to cope with this mismatch between the values espoused by his discipline and his understanding of the purposes of human activity drawn from his faith? I argue that it is not acceptable to acquiesce in the norms of the discipline and in effect compartmentalize intellectual life from spiritual life. But neither is it necessary to abandon current economic analysis and invent a totally 'new' economics. The best approach is to continue to work within the mainstream paradigm, but to remain alert to its implicit assumptions, especially in relation to policy matters. This leads to the final question in the chapter, which is how the Christian economist should proceed when it comes to policy recommendations. Two possibilities are explored. The first is the subversive approach in which the Christian economist uses the tools of economic analysis to identify some of the personal and social costs in particular policies which are often overlooked because the non-Christian economist would not look for them. The second is to adopt an explicitly Christian stance. One problem with this approach is that Christian ethics for economic life are relatively undeveloped beyond the level of generalities. So when it comes to a particular issue it may be very unclear what position to adopt. Another problem is that secular policy-makers may not be prepared to listen to advocacy based on an explicit Christian value system, arguing that this is simply inappropriate in a secular society with a variety of cultural and ethical imperatives.

Where does this leave us on the questions with which we began? The reader will have to read the chapters that follow and make up his or her own mind. However, it may stimulate that process of evaluation if I indicate where my own thinking on these matters lies. At the very least it provides a conclusion from which others may wish to dissent. The evidence seems to me to suggest that Lord Griffiths is right to argue that, in principle, the market system can accommodate a wide variety of value systems at one time without apparent strain. The problem for a Christian is simply that the sets of values that predominate in the modern market economy are very far from a Christian understanding of the purposes of economic activity. This is evident from the practical emphasis in business on maximizing shareholder value, and from the assumptions that underlie economic analysis and economic policy-making. I believe that Griffiths may be too optimistic that these secularizing forces can be countered. It requires the degree of commitment shown by the Daily Bread Co-operative or by the Amish communities to keep ourselves from the idol of materialism. Similarly, the attempt in the policy arena to introduce other values into market systems is fraught with difficulties, especially where these cut across the logic of the markets involved. The chapters by Isabella Bunn, Andrew Henley and Andrew Dilnot indicate just how difficult it is in practice to affect market outcomes in any substantial way. And Christian economists have to learn to live with ethical tensions arising from the disjunction between their personal value system and the values implicit in the analytic tools they are using every day. But then Jesus often warned that following him would be difficult, so this conclusion should not come as a surprise.

2

The culture of the market

LORD GRIFFITHS OF FFORESTFACH

I should like to begin by saying what a great pleasure it is to contribute to this volume on economic issues from a Christian perspective. The particular subject I have been asked to address is the culture of the market. It is a subject which raises difficult questions and draws on the intellectual disciplines of economics, politics, philosophy, sociology and theology. The issues raised have been debated for centuries, frequently with passion, and it goes without saying, therefore, that my contribution will be limited and modest.

Let me first say something about the expression 'the market'. Different nuances attach to its different uses. It may seem obvious but it needs saying that the market is more than simply making money. As Weber in his classic work *The Protestant Ethic and the Spirit of Capitalism* observed,

> The impulse to acquisition, pursuit of gain, of money, of the greatest possible amount of money, has in itself nothing to do with capitalism. The impulse exists and has existed among waiters, physicians, coachmen, artists, prostitutes, dishonest officials, soldiers, nobles, crusaders, gamblers and beggars. One may say that it has been common to all sorts and conditions of men at all times and in all countries of the earth.[1]

He went on to argue that the distinguishing characteristic of capitalist enterprise is the rational and continuous pursuit of profit by enterprising individuals. In the twentieth century, the characteristic institution of the market was the large corporation and the process of globalization. The growth of the international capital markets, the removal of barriers to trade, the diffusion of technological advance and cheap effective communication have spread this form of wealth creation throughout the world. In this context, the market is associated with rationality, efficiency, profit, enterprise and the large corporation.

It is important to remember that a key assumption in the thinking of Adam Smith and the eighteenth-century political philosophers through to writers such as Weber was that the market system which they analysed depended on certain values and non-market institutions for its existence. These were to be found not in the realms of commerce and economies but in philosophy, law, civil society and religion. As the title of Weber's work suggests, it was in a religious ethic that he located the ethos of capitalism.

The expression 'the market' is used in a second sense, namely as a shorthand for political economy. The last two decades have seen a concerted attempt especially in the United Kingdom and the United States to strengthen the market economy. Policies to contain the growth of government, sell off state-owned companies, reform labour markets, increase competition, reform the welfare state and foster an enterprise culture, although initially associated with Margaret Thatcher and Ronald Reagan, have now been introduced to varying degrees in many countries of the world. The reason for these policies was that the post-war consensus of large government, Keynesianism and a growing welfare state ran into all sorts of difficulty, including rising inflation occurring simultaneously with rising unemployment, the growth of an underclass and a dependency culture and the failure of government to run nationalized industries in an efficient manner. In the UK, the Labour government under Tony Blair has adopted a number of the policies of previous Conservative governments. It has given priority to maintaining an effective market economy as a foundation for dealing with economic and social issues and continued policies such as privatization, low taxes and strict fiscal and monetary discipline.

The policies of strengthening and extending the market have posed an enormous challenge to conventional wisdom. They have also created a fierce debate, especially in the area of morals, values and culture. In this context the expression 'the culture of the market' refers to the independence and robustness of people and their families, and is frequently contrasted with the dependency created by a welfare culture, epitomized by expressions such as 'get on your bike' and 'there is no such thing as society'. It is an approach which has come under sustained and passionate criticism especially from the bishops of the Anglican and Catholic Churches, theologians, academics, writers and journalists. Taken together, they have constructed a formidable litany of charges against these policies which echo previous misgivings about the market stretching back to writers such as Maurice, Ruskin, Carlyle and Scott-Holland in the nineteenth century, and Gore, Temple, Tawney and T. S. Eliot in the twentieth.

A third use of the expression 'the market' relates to the method of modern economic theory and the way in which it has penetrated the contiguous disciplines of law, politics and sociology. The market in this context is shorthand for an approach to individual decision-making based on rational self-interested behaviour in which a careful calculation is assumed of the gains and losses associated with alternative choices. Consumers are presumed to 'maximize utility' or choose a preferred pattern of consumption, subject to certain constraints such as their wealth and the price of goods and services. Firms are assumed to maximize shareholder wealth subject to the constraints of technology and regulation. This is acknowledged by economists as a highly simplified and abstract world, but nevertheless a useful basis for the derivation of the laws of supply and demand whose predictive power has proved powerful.

In the past this method was applied to economic activity to explain such phenomena as the relative size of different industries, the profitability of trade and the level of interest rates. More recently, and especially in the last thirty years, it has been applied to the behaviour of organizations ranging from political parties to the medieval church, to virtually every field of law and to issues such as marriage, surrogate mothering and the trade in body parts. Its conclusion is that all these activities are best left as unregulated free markets. In this view no area of social and political life remains outside the scope of the market, for all can be analysed through the lens of self-interest. There is not one compartment of life, the economic, which can be analysed through economic self-interest and another compartment, the personal and the social, which is a realm of trust, intimacy and caring and best analysed in social and value terms. Not surprisingly, the major issues raised by this definition of the market are the limit and appropriateness of market analysis, and the desirability or not of constructing a fence around the market so as to allow room for a public domain based on values such as honesty, neighbourliness and civility in which trust can grow.

These distinctions are important because the different uses of the term 'the market' raise different issues regarding its culture. Some may wish to defend one of the uses but not another. One use of the term is clearly more overtly political than the others. This chapter will emphasize the economic not the political, and is primarily an attempt to examine the economic culture of the market from a Christian perspective. In the next section I shall outline in more detail the criticisms which have been made of the market, then express reasons for balancing the attacks which have been made. After that I want to put forward some positive aspects of the culture of the market and then stand back and make some explicitly Christian observations.

Moral and ethical criticisms of the market

Judged by the comments of the former bishop of Durham that the market puts 'a premium on indecent and obscene greed' and that the government's restructuring of social security was 'wicked',[2] and those recently made by Professor Harvey Cox of the Harvard Divinity School that 'current thinking assigns to The Market a wisdom that in the past only gods have known',[3] one might be forgiven for thinking that the attacks on the market economy have been idiosyncratic and polemical, the stuff of good knockabout journalism but lacking substance. Nothing, however, could be further from the truth.

The 1980s saw a series of thoughtful and carefully argued publications from the churches. These included the Archbishop of Canterbury's Commission on Urban Priority Areas, *Faith in the City* (1985) and its sequel, *Living Faith in the Cities* (1990), various reports by the Church of England's Board of Social Responsibility (1987), the report of the Roman Catholic bishops of England and Wales, *The Common Good* (1996), the publication of the US Catholic bishops, *Economic Justice for All: Catholic Social Teaching and the US Economy* (1986) as well as numerous and well-publicized lectures and articles and symposia by theologians and academics such as Atherton and Plant which stressed the limits of markets and questioned or attacked government policies aimed at strengthening the market economy.[4] It also saw the publication of various reports and writings from intellectuals of a more social democratic perspective, such as Dahrendorf's *Report on Wealth Creation and Social Cohesion in a Free Society* (1995), Borrie's *Report of the Commission on Social Justice* (1994), Giddens's various writings, popularized in his book on *The Third Way* (1997) and those of Will Hutton, *The State We're In*.[5]

In their attack on the culture of the market these criticisms focus on a number of recurring themes. First, there is the charge that a market economy produces a culture of greed, hedonism and materialism with the consequent neglect of the spiritual life of the society. Archbishop Runcie speaks of the 'excessive preoccupation with prosperity and success and of monochrome values in our society' as well as 'greed, hedonism and the lust for power'.[6] This echoes the view of Tawney that

> capitalism is not so much un-Christian as anti-Christian . . . [with] . . . its emphasis on the supreme importance of material riches; the intensity of its appeal to the acquisitive appetites and the skill with which it plays on them; its worship of economic power, often with little regard to the ends which power serves or the means it uses; its idealism not merely of particular property rights but of property in general; its subordination of human beings to the exigencies, or supposed exigencies, of an economic system, as interpreted by other individuals who have a peculiar interest in interpreting them for their own advantage; its erection of divisions within the human family based on differences of income and economic circumstance . . . In such societies . . . they are commonly regarded not as vices but as virtues. To the Christian they are vices more ruinous to the soul than most of the conventional forms of immorality.[7]

It is also an attack which has come in plays, television drama, films and novels. Jacques Ellul argued that 'capitalism has subordinated all of life – individual and collective – to money' and of 'being to having'. He goes on:

> This result makes allegiance to capitalism virtually impossible for a Christian. For it is not a by-product, something that might not have happened . . . it is the inevitable consequence of capitalism, for there is no other possibility when making money becomes the purpose of life.[8]

Next, there is the charge that the market economy has produced a new individualism and a 'me-first' society, with a corresponding neglect of common values and an erosion of mutual obligation and sense of solidarity within society. The distinguished journalist, Clifford Longley, writing from a Catholic perspective, quotes approvingly the papal encyclical *Quadragesimo Anno*: 'The right ordering of economic life cannot be left to a free competition of forces. From this source as from a poisoned spring have originated and spread all the errors of individualistic economic teaching.'[9] For Longley free markets are definitely a poisoned spring or, as he prefers to describe them, structures of sin: 'the church's social teaching explicitly rejects belief in the automatic beneficence of market forces and insists that the end result of market forces must be scrutinized and if necessary corrected in the name of natural law, social justice, human rights and the common good.'[10]

The concept of the common good, which can be traced back to the attempt by Thomas Aquinas to integrate Aristotelian theory with that of the early church fathers, is crucial to understanding the Catholic case against individualism, and in particular the deeply ingrained scepticism which papal encyclicals over the twentieth century showed towards capitalism. The common good is the shared values of a society which acknowledges not only the interests and well-being of each individual, body and soul, but also the good of everyone in that society. When people recognize their interdependence and commit themselves to be responsible for the good of each individual and the good of all, they will be acting in solidarity with each other. This is saying in no uncertain terms that there most certainly is such a thing as society and that society is undermined by a market economy in which people primarily pay attention to their own interests.

Writing from a different perspective but nevertheless expressing similar sentiments, John Gray has launched a formidable attack on market-driven economic change, claiming that unconstrained market institutions will undermine social and political stability because they impose on the population unprecedented levels of economic insecurity, threatening devastation to families and communities. The constant change demanded by market reforms undermines authority and tradition, with 'a concomitant metamorphosis of moral judgment into a species of personal preferences, between which reason is powerless to arbitrate'.[11]

Third, there is the charge that the market economy produces

growing inequality in the distribution of income and either creates poverty or at least allows it to grow. In recent years the litmus test among churchmen in judging the morality of a society has been its attitude to the poor; the title of David Sheppard's book *Bias to the Poor* and the Roman Catholic notion of 'the preferential option for the poor' both express what many contemporary theologians argue is the only approach consistent with a proper biblical understanding.[12] The Catholic bishops of England and Wales have argued that the market involves an 'option against the poor', so throwing great doubt on a trickle-down theory of wealth creation, which holds that a process of sustained wealth creation in an economy will have a beneficial impact for all groups in society including the least well-off.[13] This concern with inequality and social cohesion was at the heart of the Dahrendorf and Borrie reports.

The empirical evidence does suggest that the deregulated and increasingly competitive market economy of the kind we have seen in Britain has resulted in a growing divergence between the incomes of the well-paid and those of service workers, a growing gulf between the rich and the poor and the growth of an underclass from which people find it difficult to escape. It has been documented in various reports, especially by the Rowntree Foundation.[14] John Gray not only argues that the bolstering of the market has been an engine creating poverty but that the growth of crime results directly from such policies.[15] At the same time, welfare reforms have put pressure on the least well-off who feel further ground down by the revival of the market system.

Another criticism levelled against the market is that it is constantly extending its boundaries. The economic culture of the market is no longer confined to the business sector. It has invaded the world of schools, with poor performing schools run by companies, the world of television, with TV licences being auctioned, the world of medicine, with the creation of an internal market between purchasers (doctors and health authority) and providers (hospital), and care for the elderly with nursing homes run by private companies not local authorities. The disabled seeking help, the elderly seeking care and patients seeking hospital admission have all become customers seeking services. The language of business, such as developing strategic objectives, cost-benefit analysis, market-testing and outsourcing is changing the nature of the public services. To meet business objectives the teacher is under pressure to reduce the time allocated to individual pupils, and the doctor the time that can be given to see individual patients. The concept of education being about the development of the whole person has been distorted into teaching merely to pass exams; and the concept of health being about the personal care of the patient has become the management of budgets and the achievement of output targets for such things as hip replacements and heart operations. The traditions on which the professions were based have given way to a managerial culture based on contracts and market exchange. Extending the boundaries of the market economy has transformed the nature of our society.

A fifth criticism of the market is the risk it takes frequently on the basis of short-term profit. For nearly four decades the environment has rightly been highlighted as an area at risk, in which the exercise of trusteeship and stewardship has been seriously neglected, with business frequently being in the dock. More recently, in the controversy over 'mad-cow' disease and genetically modified foods, the role of companies has been again placed under the searchlight. The interests of shareholders are perceived as paramount, while those of the consumer and the general public are relegated to second place.

Finally, there is the charge which comes out especially in the work of Giddens and Gray that the neo-liberal advocacy of extending the market and its culture is fundamentally inconsistent with a devotion to such conservative institutions as the traditional family and the nation.[16] The argument for extending greater choice in the economic sphere and in the provision of public services may or may not be valid, but it cannot suddenly cease to have validity when we discuss the family or the nation. It is alleged to be a wholly arbitrary method of proceeding. A conservative disposition is cautious and pragmatic in its approach to change, placing great emphasis on tradition which has embodied the wisdom of past experience. But a market society will undermine traditional structures of authority as well as the communities in which their traditions are held, so rendering ineffective those values which support traditional ways of life.

I have outlined these criticisms of market culture at considerable length, partly to show the breadth of the criticism but also to show the intensity of feeling from diverse critics such as Tawney, Ellul and Runcie. Taken together, these ethical and moral criticisms of the market constitute a formidable attack on its culture which cannot, whatever our inclinations, be treated lightly. To the extent that they are theological, they come from a well-developed theology dealing with poverty, injustice, the common good and materialism. It is a theology which has paid great regard to changes in the distribution of income. Judged within this framework the market has been weighed in the balances and found wanting.

Reservations about the moral critique of the market

I have a number of reservations about this approach. The first derives from the real achievements of the market economy in creating wealth and employment which are less emphasized by critics of the market. Although there is dispute among economic historians as to what happened in the earlier phase of the industrial revolution, the evidence since the mid-nineteenth century and especially since the Second World War points to unprecedented rises in the material standard of living of large numbers of people in market economies, with corresponding rises in life expectancy and standards of health. In recent decades the market-orientated nature of the US economy has been an engine in creating jobs compared with the sluggishness of the much more regulated and inflexible continental European economies which have fared much less well. Between 1982 and 1998, employment grew in the USA by 1.6 per cent per year, but in European Union countries (excluding the UK) by only 0.3 per cent. From a roughly comparable base (employment in the USA in 1982 was 99.5 million and in EU countries, excluding the UK, 107.1 million), 31.9 million jobs were created in the USA compared with 5.3 million in EU countries. One major factor in accounting for this is the rigid labour market of the EU countries and the bias towards safety nets and welfare. Or consider the policy of privatization, the sale of state-owned and managed companies, which was introduced less than twenty years ago in the UK and has now been adopted by well over one hundred countries: by removing the political constraints of managing a business, allowing greater freedom over pricing and investment decisions, the development of a business strategy and a service-orientated culture, privatization has resulted in increasing productivity and performance. It is considered by many countries and international organizations an unambiguous success. By contrast, the other major alternative put forward as an engine to drive wealth creation, namely state-ownership and planning, has proved a failure, and has even been discarded in countries such as China.

I make this point on the historical record of the market for two reasons: the creation of wealth is important to the well-being of society and should not be ignored or brushed aside; in addition, we should not presume that wealth creation somehow can be automatically taken for granted. Different economic systems provide different economic incentives, which have quite different consequences for wealth creation and job creation.

A second reservation is that the criticisms of the market which I have outlined can be dated to the nineteenth century. They are reflected in the novels of Dickens, the poetry of Blake and in such tomes as Engels, *The Condition of the Working Class in England* (1845) and the writings of Marx. The impact of markets in eighteenth-century literature, as Albert Hirschman has pointed out, was different. Quite apart from the effect that the expansion of commerce was expected to have in restraining the arbitrary use of power by the sovereign, it was also considered to have a beneficial impact on the citizen and civil society. For example, Montesquieu in the *Spirit of the Laws* (1748) states that 'it is almost a general rule that wherever there is commerce, manners are gentle',[17] a sentiment which is reflected in the writings of others such as Condorcet and Thomas Paine.

David Hume and Adam Smith emphasized that commerce brought out such virtues as industriousness, assiduity, frugality, punctuality and probity. Frequently, the precise way in which commerce had this beneficial effect was not made clear but occasional writers such as Samuel Ricard did make it more explicit:

> Commerce attaches men to one another through mutual utility. Through commerce the moral and physical passions are superseded by interest. Commerce has a special character which distinguishes it from all other professions. It affects the feelings of men so strongly that it makes him who was proud and haughty suddenly turn supple, bending and serviceable. Through commerce man learns to deliberate, to be

> honest, to acquire manners, to be prudent and reserved in both talk and action. Sensing the necessity to be wise in order to succeed, he frees vice, or at least his demeanor exhibits decency and seriousness so as not to arouse any adverse judgment on the part of present and future acquaintances; he would not dare make a spectacle of himself for fear of damaging his credit standing and thus society may well avoid a scandal which it might otherwise have to deplore.[18]

The benefits claimed for the market here are significant and they need to be set against the later criticisms.

A third reason for my reservation is my own personal experience in the City of London for over thirty years and my being or having been a non-executive director of more than ten companies both in Britain and the USA. The world of business seen from the inside as a player is very different from the criticisms made by those who stand on the touchline or, better, in the grandstand as spectators. I observe executives of companies placing great emphasis on finding ways of helping people develop their potential, paying a great deal of attention to ways of training people, wrestling with issues of fairness and equity in compensation and ownership, setting out business principles, codes of conduct and sets of explicit standards and devoting a good deal of thought to developing a culture for the company. This seems a dimension which is totally neglected in the litany of charges brought against the market. I have no doubt that certain charges against the market carry weight, but as they stand they are in great danger of being unbalanced and wrong. They need correction.

Christianity and market culture

For the market to be properly examined within a Christian context we need not only a theology of justice and poverty, but also a theology of wealth creation. The reason why many Christians are one-sided in their view on the market economy is the lack of any such theory. There are attempts, suggestions and tentative moves in this direction. But a theology of wealth creation which could be of use in tempering these criticisms simply does not exist. It is important therefore to examine some of the building blocks of the economic culture of a market economy within a Christian perspective. This is not in any way meant to be a theology of wealth creation, but it does consist of certain observations which might be considered useful for such an exercise.

One insight has to do with human creativity and the significance of inventiveness and innovation. Any Christian world-view must begin with God the Creator. The Bible starts with the declaration: 'In the beginning God created the heavens and the earth' (Genesis 1: 1). The physical universe, the animal and plant kingdoms are part of an extraordinarily complex created order. The supreme act of creation, however, was that of man, made 'in the image and likeness of God'. Philip Wogaman suggests that 'the doctrine of creation may finally prove decisive as the foundation for ethics' because through it 'we express our understanding of how it is that God is concretely related to the actual events and structures of this world'.[19] The human potential for self-reflection, imagination, logical thought, experimentation and discovery – in other words, everything that we would associate with creativity – derives from our being created by God. Our vocation given by God is to exercise 'dominion' over the visible world, to 'subdue' the earth. Man as creator, therefore, is more than simply a creature of nature or product of society: he shares with God the ongoing task of creation. As the papal encyclical *Laborem Exercens* makes clear,

> The word of God's revelation is profoundly marked by the fundamental truth that man, created in the image of God, shares by his work in the creativity of the Creator and that, within the limits of his own human capabilities, man in a sense continues to develop that activity and perfects it as he advances further and further in the discovery of the resources and values contained in the whole of creation.[20]

Michael Novak has taken this concept of creativity further by using the insights of the philosopher Bernard Lonergan.[21] The world as Lonergan views it is neither complete nor stable. Events which happen are not entirely random, so we are not foolish to ascribe probabilities to their occurrence. The world, in other words, is not cold, rational, geometric, always behaving in a logical and predictable way: but nor is it totally irrational, random, without any pattern. 'Nature is not to be regarded as achieved, complete, finished. Creation is unfinished.'[22] Innovation, invention and enterprise depend on a mindset which views the world in terms of emergent probabilities. With this view of the world processes, the insights of the entrepreneur will result in fresh discoveries, pioneering efforts. The great insight of Adam Smith was that the expanding wealth of a nation depended not on its natural resources, size of population, role of the state or military, but on the extent to which its system (he called it the natural system of liberty) would through exchange unleash human creativity.

I am not for one moment suggesting that human creativity is confined to a market economy, as is abundantly clear from the record of the Soviet Union and Nazi Germany. But as far as creativity in the world of work and business is concerned, creativity as a response to the perceived needs and wants of consumers, companies, investors, governments and trusts, the market order encourages innovation and development more than other systems. The reason is the respect it has for the talent and potential of the entrepreneur. Path-breaking research and new advances in science will not benefit society unless they are transformed into products and services which can be produced by companies using capital and offering a return to their shareholders. The entrepreneur as the embodiment of creativity used in the service of others is key to a market system. In the encyclical, *Sollicitudo Rei Socialis*, Pope John Paul II identifies what he terms 'a right of economic initiative' and links it to 'the creative subjectivity of the citizen', which is I believe an important step in recognizing the value of the entrepreneur.[23]

The relentless quest by entrepreneurs to finance new ideas with talented teams of people is not confined to the Silicon Valley frontier of the technological revolution in information technology. It is apparent in the extent of innovation in global capital markets, new approaches to management services, different methods of distribution to the customer and so on. Another characteristic of market culture is what Weber termed rationality. Although he argued that capitalism had existed in many cultures previously, the defining feature of modern capitalism was 'the rational capitalist organization of free labour'.[24] Rationality meant the relentless quest for the optimum, which resulted in rules and strict processes in which the industrial organization became a bureaucracy. We now associate market culture with words such as efficiency, calculability, quantification, predictability and control. It is important to recognize that the concept of rationality which lies behind efficiency is part of the Christian world-view that he associated with a reformed theology. In this view magic and superstition had been eliminated in explaining the natural world and salvation, and the believer was called to develop a Christian mind to which his will and emotions were subservient. This emphasis on the importance of the mind led to an ordered and purposeful view of his life and it was natural, therefore, to carry over the same outlook into the world of business, in which the individual was a trustee of God-given talents and opportunities with the responsibility to use them to good effect.

Weber realized, however, that rationality had another side. The resourceful and enterprising individual could become imprisoned through industrial bureaucracy in an iron cage of rationality with profoundly dehumanizing consequences. F. W. Taylor's creation of scientific management meant that employees carried out only a few tasks in the production process, with most of their skills and abilities remaining unused, and Henry Ford's development of large factories with automated assembly lines which involved huge hierarchical and bureaucratic organizations, in which complex operational manuals were developed in order to minimize initiative and flexibility of response on the part of the worker, seems to have justified Weber's analysis.[25]

One of the observations which led to the charge of the dehumanizing effects of the market – especially from the liberation theologians of Latin America – was the image of people used as alternatives to parts of machines in highly automated mass-production manufacturing. As Henry Ford said, 'Why is it that I get the whole person when all I want is a pair of hands?' It is no surprise that this form of industrial organization bred powerful trade unions which were intent on defining the job very precisely, minimizing the hours worked, resulting in poor industrial relations. This culture, however, was doomed to collapse through the weight of its own rigidities. It resulted in overmanning, high costs, and it proved to be very difficult for management to introduce change. When Toyota started re-engineering their production of cars in the 1960s through just-in-time production, they embarked on a wholly new approach which empowered blue-collar workers effectively to run the factory floor without the supervision of middle management. It took tremendous courage and drew on great resources of trust between employees.[26]

More generally, the move from an industrial to a post-industrial society associated with the decline of manufacturing and the growth of service industries and new technologies has led to a typical post-industrial organization with a number of distinct characteristics. These include a flat organizational structure, a more fluid and integrated relationship between parts of the organization, the delegation of responsibility to people well down in the organization, less of an emphasis on rules and more on the internalization of the organization's culture and an emphasis on the creativity and total resource of people. The significance of the knowledge worker to the organization has meant greater emphasis on training, the design of the job to fit the individual and considerable care over the design of a compensation system. Today's information revolution demands not only new types of companies but the restructuring of large companies so as to create internal markets within their own distinctive organizational cultures, which can offer a challenge to smaller, flexible more mobile organizations growing up around them. I find many of these developments, especially as they strengthen the significance of the individual, exciting. To the extent that they are part of a relentless quest for efficiency, they stem from a mindset in which reason and purpose are part of Christian stewardship.

Another consideration of market culture has to do with communities and values. The concept of community, of individuals being persons who need each other rather than isolated automatons, is the essence of a Trinitarian view of creation. Man is naturally and incurably social. Society is made up of communities or mediating structures, the family, school, village, neighbourhood, clubs, churches and so on. Personal well-being depends on individuals being part of different communities. One important set of communities is related to the market. Production and distribution take place through partnerships, small businesses, exchanges, trade associations and the large publicly traded corporation: the idea of the market being impersonal and highly individualistic could not be further from the truth. The modern corporation is a community based on trust and underpinned typically by a strong statement of values. More than two decades ago Peters and Waterman found that companies which emphasized shared values performed more successfully than those which did not. Further work on corporate culture and performance has confirmed the significance of culture in influencing performance and the need for leadership which is decisive, visionary and energetic to lead cultural change. Kotter and Heskett from Harvard, in a detailed study of this subject, conclude by emphasizing the values necessary for success.

> If our economic organizations are going to live up to their potential, we must find, develop and encourage more people to lead in the service of others. Without leadership firms cannot adapt to a fast moving world. But if leaders do not have the hearts of servants the result is tyranny.[27]

It is because business executives recognize the need for business principles and an explicit set of values at the heart of their companies that companies have become such important carriers of values in our society.

A further insight of the market has to do with opportunity, especially in the context of inequality and poverty. Even though poverty may always be with us, the Christian following the example of Christ has a special responsibility to help the disadvantaged and those who have been made poor. Governments have an important part to play in the provision of welfare and it would be hard at present to imagine anyone who could provide an adequate substitute for government.

But even here the market may help. One of the major causes of measured poverty in the UK is unemployment. We know that sustained economic growth in the context of a dynamic economy is probably the best source of job creation that we have – hence the contrast between the US and EU economies. Policies, therefore, which encourage markets will foster job creation and once in work even the lowest paid have the opportunity to enhance their position and avoid being swept into the underclass. I believe that a competitive market will allow employees choice, will reduce discrimination and will, especially in the service industries, spur firms to enhance training. The market economy which creates private wealth abounds in trusts, foundations and charities, many of which are geared to fighting poverty and strengthening opportunity. This is not the complete answer by any means, but it is a part.

A fifth aspect of market culture is what Weber termed its ethos. The dominant ethos of a competitive market is service to customers, responsibility to employees, suppliers and the communities in which they operate and accountability to shareholders and regulators. Competition requires of firms that they make a priority of their customers: and nowhere is this more clearly seen than among companies in the service sector. The act of service is valuable in itself, but it also has one particularly strong implication. Two great costs of running a service business are the turnover of customers and the turnover of staff. The two are not unrelated. Research undertaken at the Harvard Business School has shown that the value chain of a service business starts with the customers' evaluation of the front-line staff, which in turn depends on the employees' satisfaction in the job, which in turn depends on not just their compensation but the backup they receive and in particular the training they can get. A low rate of turnover in front-line staff will mean a low rate of turnover of customers. Hence the need in any service business to help front-line staff develop.

Perspectives on the culture of the market

It is now time to bring together some of the themes in this chapter. The starting-point is the distinctive Christian legitimacy of markets within the economic order. This is an argument which involves a number of steps. Step one is the recognition that the physical world is part of the created order and that God's mandate is for humankind to exercise dominion and take control of it in a responsible manner. It is by carrying out this mandate that we develop agriculture to produce food and clothes, construct buildings in which to live and work and harness the resources of the world for our well-being. The world is God's, we are his trustees and wealth is his blessing for us all. Step two acknowledges that we have been created, *imago Dei*, as responsible and enterprising people with the need and drive to work, so that the creation of wealth is both seen as the reward of diligence and again explicitly recognized as the favour of God. Step three recognizes that, in the world as it is, private property has been given the full support of the moral law so that the rewards of hard work, risk-taking and saving are protected for the person and their family.

The existence of markets through which people engage in voluntary exchange to the benefit of both parties is the inevitable outcome of the three steps which I have outlined. Markets as part of the economic order have a legitimacy which is rooted in creation and the covenant. From the criticisms of the market made by people such as Tawney, Ellul and Bonino, it seems as if the whole market structure is an inhuman, exploitative, evil system with which the Christian can have no truck. This I believe is fundamentally misconceived: markets have a legitimacy in a Judaeo-Christian framework which is based on the creation mandate, the nature of work and the protection of property. An interesting conjecture in the correction is whether we should accord to markets a similar place to that which we give the family and the state in Judaeo-Christian theology. Markets are deeply rooted in the biblical understanding of the creation, and are essential to expressing freedom and choice. They are open to abuse, but so is the family and so is the state. Any economic order which systematically seeks to suppress the freedom of markets will be one which also systematically denies human rights.

But legitimacy does not imply autonomy. One of the problems for a Christian in defending the benefits of the market is that its leading proponents in recent decades, such as Friedman, Becker and most of all Hayek, have constructed the case for free markets within a thoroughly secular framework, in which the market is an autonomous process, wholly independent of any created order or revealed morality. Hayek's starting-point is the observation that social reality is so complex and 'unknowable' that the contemporary social and economic order is not the conscious product of the design of any one individual. Rather it is the result of a process of cultural evolution in which those habits and practices and institutions which have increased the chances of the survival of the group have flourished. This has produced what he calls a spontaneous order, which Adam Smith well understood in terms of the 'invisible hand', which leads entrepreneurs to promote an end which was not part of the individual's self-interested actions. This process has found its most complete development in the open society of Western industrialized democracies which he refers to by the word 'catallaxy', which is derived from the Greek verb *Katallattein*, and which Hayek understands as meaning to exchange, to admit into the community and to change from enemy to friend.

A spontaneous order required people to hold ethical values, but these have emerged through the process of biological and cultural evolution. 'The important point', says Hayek,

> is that every man growing up in a given culture will find in himself rules – and will recognize the actions of others as conforming or not conforming to various rules. This is, of course, not proof that they are a permanent or unalterable part of 'human nature' or that they are innate, but proof only that they are part of a cultural heritage that is likely to be fairly constant.[28]

This is tempered by the fact that these rules will change with the stage reached by society. When we were organized in small tribes, then the value of solidarity and altruism were relevant, but in the catallaxy of the free market they have been replaced through evolution by commercial morals. A similar emphasis is made by the Friedmans, who acknowledge their debt to Hayek: 'A society's values, its culture, its social conventions – all these developed in the same way, through voluntary exchange, spontaneous co-operation, the evolution of a complex structure through trial and error, acceptance and rejection . . . a kind of social evolution paralleling biological evolution.'[29]

The idea of the autonomy of the free market as part of a spontaneous economic, cultural, political and social system goes well beyond the boundaries of economics and carries enormous implications: it is a rejection of the idea of transcendent and absolute moral standards, it is heavily biased against any kind of intervention in the market and it has no basis for placing certain activities outside the scope of markets. It is because it is ultimately a thoroughly humanistic analysis that it cannot be defended within a Judaeo-Christian theology: as a result it must be rejected. The irony is that, at the end of his three volumes *Law, Legislation and Liberty*, Hayek wrote an epilogue on the sources of human values, attacking in particular the views of Marx and Freud; the one because of a belief in egalitarianism and the other because of psychiatry's attempt to free us from repression and conventional morals by abandoning the concepts of good and evil, right and wrong, but both of which undermine the free society.[30]

Finally, something must be said on avarice, materialism and Mammon. In posing the choice between money and wealth, Jesus personifies and deifies money with the use of the expression Mammon. This was a choice faced by the nomadic Israelites in the

Sinai desert: it was the same choice faced by those who listened to the teachings of Jesus centuries later; and it was the choice faced by the early church. It has been a choice for the last two centuries and is as important a choice today as ever. For countries which feel the weight of secularism and post-modernism, and which have rejected a personal God and a created world, it is a choice which will be made in favour of hedonism and materialism. While I do not believe the market is neutral, in that it clearly has a bias in favour of efficiency, profit and service, nor do I believe that a market system *per se* has a bias to materialism.

At the end of his seminal work, Weber quotes Baxter's view, that wealth should lie on the shoulders of a saint like a light cloak, with his own view that the spirit of religious asceticism had escaped from the iron cage, leaving it to be filled by the ghosts of dead religious beliefs.[31] It can be read as an obituary or it can be taken as a call to action.

My conclusions, therefore, are that markets have a legitimacy within a Christian world-view; that we must reject their defence as autonomous of morality; that they form an important building block for a theology of wealth creation; that in any system there will always be a choice between God or Mammon; and that the market economy is an open society with great opportunities for Christian leadership.

Notes

1 Max Weber, *The Protestant Ethic and the Spirit of Capitalism* (London, 1992), 6.

2 Paul Heelas and Paul Morris, *The Values of the Enterprise Culture* (London, 1992), 12.

3 Harvey Cox, 'The market as God', *Atlantic Monthly* (March 1999).

4 Archbishop of Canterbury's Commission on Urban Priority Areas, *Faith in the City* (London, 1985); Archbishop of Canterbury's Advisory Group on Priority Areas, *Living Faith in the Cities* (London, 1990); *The Common Good* (London, 1996); Catholic Bishops Conference of England and Wales, *Economic Justice for All: Catholic Social Teaching and the US Economy* (Washington, 1986); John Atherton, *Christianity and the Market* (London, 1992); Raymond Plant, 'Enterprise in its place: the moral limits of markets', in Heelas and Morris, *Values of Enterprise Culture*.

5 Ralf Dahrendorf, *Report on Wealth Creation and Social Cohesion in a Free*

Society (London, 1995); Commission on Social Justice, 'Social justice: strategies for national renewal', *Vintage* (October 1994); Anthony Giddens, *The Third Way* (Cambridge, 1998); Will Hutton, *The State We're In* (London, 1995).

6 Robert Runcie, *Panorama* interview, cited by F. Mount, *Daily Telegraph* (1 April 1988) and speech to the Global Survival Conference, Oxford, *Daily Telegraph* (12 April 1988).

7 R. H. Tawney, 'A note on Christianity and the social order', *The Attack and Other Papers* (London, 1953).

8 Jacques Ellul, *Money and Power* (Downers Grove, IL, 1984), 20.

9 Pope Pius XI, *Quadragesimo Anno* (1931), para. 88.

10 Clifford Longley, 'Structures of sin and the free market: John Paul II on capitalism', in Paul Vallely (ed.), *The New Politics* (London, 1998).

11 John Gray and David Willetts, *Is Conservatism Dead?* (London, 1997).

12 David Sheppard, *Bias to the Poor* (London, 1983).

13 Catholic Bishops Conference of England and Wales, *The Common Good and the Catholic Church's Social Teaching* (London, 1996).

14 Peter M. Barclay and John Hills, *Joseph Rowntree Foundation Inquiry into Income and Wealth* (York, 1995).

15 Gray and Willetts, *Is Conservatism Dead?*, 6.

16 Giddens, *Third Way*, 15; Gray and Willetts, *Is Conservatism Dead?*, 27.

17 Charles Louis Montesquieu, *De l'esprit des lois* (Paris, [1748] 1961), quoted in A. O. Hirschman, 'Rival interpretations of market society: civilizing, destructive or feeble?', *Journal of Economic Literature*, 20 (December 1982).

18 Samuel Ricard, *Traité général du commerce* (Amsterdam, 1781), cited by Hirschman, 'Rival interpretations'.

19 Quoted in John Atherton, *Christianity and the Market* (London, 1992).

20 *Laborem Exercens* (1982).

21 Michael Novak, *The Spirit of Democratic Capitalism* (New York, 1982).

22 Ibid., ch. 3.

23 *Sollicitudo Rei Socialis* (1987).

24 Max Weber, *The Protestant Ethic and the Spirit of Capitalism* (London, 1992).

25 F. W. Taylor, *The Principles of Scientific Management* (New York, 1911).

26 James P. Womack, Daniel T. Jones and Daniel Ross, *The Machine that Changed the World* (New York, 1991).

27 John P. Kotter and James L. Heskett, *Corporate Culture and Performance* (New York, 1992).

28 F. A. Hayek, *Law, Legislation and Liberty, i: Rules and Order* (London, 1973), 19.

29 Milton and Rose Friedman, *Free to Choose* (London, 1980).

30 F. A. Hayek, *Law, Legislation and Liberty*, iii (London, 1979), epilogue.

31 Weber, *Protestant Ethic.*

3

Does shareholder value drive the world?

DAVID NUSSBAUM

Introduction

An American businesswoman was at the pier of a small coastal Mexican village when a small boat with just one fisherman docked. Inside the small boat were several large yellowfin fish. The American complimented the Mexican on the quality of his fish and asked how long it took to catch them. The Mexican replied that it took only a little while. The American asked why he did not stay out longer and catch more fish. The Mexican said he had enough to support his family's immediate needs. The American then asked what he did with the rest of his time. The Mexican fisherman smiled and replied, 'Well, I sleep late, fish a little, play with my children, take a siesta with my wife Maria, stroll into the village each evening where I drink some wine and play the guitar with my amigos; I have a full and busy life, you know.'

The American scoffed, 'Not only am I an economist, but I have an MBA as well; and I could help you. You should spend more time fishing and with the proceeds buy a bigger boat; and with the larger catch that would allow you to make, you could buy several boats, eventually you would have a fleet of fishing boats. Instead of selling your catch to a middleman you would sell directly to the processor, in due course opening your own canneries, here and abroad. You would control the product, the processing and the distribution. You could leave this small coastal fishing village and move to Mexico City, maybe ultimately to New York City, from where you would run your expanding enterprise, which would employ many people.'

The Mexican fisherman looked interested, and asked, 'And how long will all this take?' The American replied, 'Oh, about fifteen to twenty years.' 'And then what, Señorita?' enquired the

Mexican. The American laughed, 'That's the best part. When the time is right, you would announce that the company was to be floated on the stock-market, and sell your shares to the public and become very rich. You would make millions.' 'Ah, millions indeed?', said the Mexican; 'and then what?' 'Then', the American responded, 'Then you could retire. Move to a small coastal village, where you could sleep late, fish a little, play with your grandchildren, take a siesta with your wife, stroll into the village each evening where you could drink some wine and play the guitar with your amigos.' 'Fascinating', smiled the Mexican, as he ambled home.

We are all on the side of the Mexican, of course. Yet here we are: I have spent some hours away from my family and friends to research and write this chapter, and now you are spending some of your time reading it, when you could be strolling towards a wine-bar in which to spend the evening with your friends.

In our story, the American was introducing the Mexican to the idea of creating value – and indeed jobs – through enterprise and growth, taking his business into the world of global capital markets and realizing value from his shareholding to enjoy in his retirement. In this chapter, we look at shareholder value, and consider: What is it? Why is it happening? What effects does it have? What might God make of it? And how should we relate to it? In all of this, we will be trying to link these matters to the contemporary culture of economics. Francis Fukuyama in his book, *Trust: The Social Virtues and the Creation of Prosperity*, wrote: 'Economic life is deeply embedded in social life, and it cannot be understood apart from the customs, morals and habits of the society in which it occurs. In short, it cannot be divorced from culture.'[1]

Before we look at shareholder value, there are two key points to note and a disclosure of potential conflict of interest to make. First, in the physical sciences, theories cannot change the phenomena to which they relate; physical nature, unlike humans, follows its course irrespective of what theories relate to it, and so things are generally not changed by the ideas that are propounded about them. So whether we know about or believe in gravity makes no difference to the way an apple falls. In contrast, in social sciences, such as economics, what is believed makes a difference; so much so, indeed, that theories can be effective without being valid. This is because participants in economic activities base their decisions on expectations about the future; but the future which they are trying to anticipate is itself dependent on the decisions they are taking today, and on the decisions of other actors who are also trying to anticipate the decisions which they and all the participants will be taking. So if they believe, for example, that globalization will continue, business managers may make different decisions than they would have done had they not held such a belief. If those decisions foster the globalization phenomenon, a positive feedback loop is created, which for a time, maybe a long time, can be self-supporting.

George Soros, the renowned financier and philanthropist who has made a great deal of money from participating in financial markets, calls this phenomenon 'reflexivity', and distinguishes it from the traditional 'equilibrium' concept in classical economic models.[2] Does all this matter? I think it does: the existence of widely accepted theory based on the paradigm of economically driven individuals seeking to maximize their utility may provide powerful analytical and predictive tools. When it becomes an ideology, it may in the end also encourage precisely that kind of behaviour which it assumes, but which might otherwise be less prevalent. In particular, economic values and models may penetrate into areas of society that were not previously governed by economic values, such as politics, medicine and family relationships. This extension of the economic approach into everything is challenged by the response which Jesus gave, when tempted to go for an economic version of salvation, that 'humanity should not live on the basis of material utility alone, but on the full provision of God in creation', to translate roughly the traditional words, 'Man shall not live on bread alone, but on every word that comes from the mouth of God' (Matthew 4: 4, quoting Deuteronomy 8: 3).

Secondly, we should, I believe, acknowledge our own agendas and economic interests in these matters. People like me who are invited to write chapters like this are likely to be privileged people. I do *not* mean in the sense of, 'it is a privilege to be asked to contribute to a collection of chapters from such eminent people by such a prestigious publisher'. Rather, I mean that I have had the educational opportunities to engage in this sort of activity, and been fortunate enough to have an interesting career in my work. I dare even to go further: you, as a reader of material such as this, are at least very probably amongst the privileged of the world. Few of us could properly describe ourselves as 'under-privileged'.

So we might think carefully about the words of Reinhold Niebuhr:

> The moral attitudes of dominant and privileged groups are characterized by universal self-deception and hypocrisy . . . the intelligence of privileged groups is usually applied to the task of inventing specious proofs for the theory that universal values spring from, and that general interests are served by, the special privileges which they hold.[3]

One risk is that we will come to think that we deserve the privileges we enjoy; after all, we are entitled to them for all the work and study that we have undertaken. We may indeed be entitled to them, but that is not at all the same as saying that we deserve them. If I were to buy a lottery ticket, and my numbers came up in the draw, I would be entitled to the winnings; but that does not mean I would deserve them.

So what about the disclosure of potential conflicts of interest? Our thinking about matters like shareholder value is likely to be influenced by our experience of life, and especially by the decisions we have taken and the choices we have made. For example, I think that perhaps you as a reader should know that I have done very well out of shareholder value; and that might just influence how I think about it, and so what I write about it. I am not going to divulge too many personal details, but I will tell you that, because of the gains I have made through working in a shareholder value context, my family does not have a mortgage on the comfortable semi-detached house we live in, and we do have some savings, and the prospect of a pension. On the other hand, I now work for an organization which is instinctively critical of shareholder value. So, let the reader beware! Indeed, I encourage you to think about such questions in relation to anyone whose thinking you take account of, especially on economic matters: for in my view, how we live interacts with how we think, as well as vice versa. Those of us who are Christians should be especially alert to this, for ours is a faith which I suggest is as much about *orthopraxis*, right living, as it is about *orthodoxy*, right belief.

Shareholder value

1. What is shareholder value?

Shareholder value is, naturally enough, the value that a shareholder obtains from owning that share. Shareholder value theory, or the shareholder value philosophy, however, goes rather further than that. In its pure form, it can be captured in the claim that *the ultimate or primary purpose of a company is to maximize the value it creates for its shareholders*. In 1995 and 1996 the *Financial Times* ran a twenty-part series on 'Mastering Management'. The finance sections of that series were summarized in seven basic principles, the first of which was, 'Management acts in the interests of the shareholders to maximise the current value of the company'.[4]

The alternative view is generally regarded as being the 'stakeholder' approach. This views a business as having obligations to a range of stakeholders: typically, customers, employees, suppliers and the community, as well as shareholders. For example, George Merck, founder of the large and profitable pharmaceutical company Merck, set out the company's approach explicitly: 'We try never to forget that medicine is for the people. It is not for the profits' – though profits there have certainly been. Henry Ford argued that running a company was about more than making profits:

> I do not believe that we should make such an awful profit on our cars. A reasonable profit is right, but not too much. So it has been my policy to force the price of the car down as fast as production would permit, and give the benefits to the users and the labourers, with surprisingly enormous benefits to ourselves.

Another example is the Japanese firm Sony, whose founding prospectus described its purpose as 'creating an ideal workplace, free, dynamic and joyous, where dedicated engineers will be able to realize their craft and skills at the highest possible level' and explained that 'we shall eliminate any untoward profit-seeking' – though this did not stop much profit being made.

The shareholder value philosophy, however, is not new. Some forty years ago, the economist Milton Friedman wrote:

> [T]here is one and only one social responsibility of business – to use its resources and engage in activities designed to increase its profits. Few

> trends could so thoroughly undermine the very foundations of our free society as the acceptance by corporate officials of a social responsibility other than to make as much money for their stockholders as possible. This is a fundamentally subversive doctrine.[5]

More recently, writing in another *Financial Times* series, on 'Mastering Strategy', James P. Walsh from the University of Michigan Business School characterized prevalent views as being that 'The purpose of the company is to make money for its owners. Any talk that distracts from this goal is tantamount to corporate treason.'[6] Today, the shareholder value approach is widely accepted, confidently promulgated and robustly defended.

2. Why is the shareholder value approach happening?

There are four factors which I identify as key reasons why chief executives and others are worshipping at the altar of shareholder value.

Academic and management theory

Modern financial economics provides a coherent, consistent and robust theoretical basis for the shareholder value philosophy. Contemporary corporate finance is a well-thought-out, thorough and rigorous subject, and some of the best brains in the world are devoted to developing, testing and applying it. As in other subjects, once a particular orthodoxy becomes established, it tends to be assumed. So Professors Dick Brealey and Stewart Myers in their *Principles of Corporate Finance*, one of the standard academic textbooks, explain in the first chapter: 'Most of the time we assume that the financial manager acts to increase the value of the shareholders' investment in the firm.'[7] (And what is excepted by that qualification 'most of the time' is the problem of conflicts of interest between owners and managers, known as 'agency theory', which is summarized on page 917!)

Writers whose work crosses between the academics and the practitioners also take shareholder value as the explicit intellectual foundation for their work. Three partners of the leading international business consultants McKinsey & Co. published *Valuation: Measuring and Managing the Value of Companies*. The book says it is aimed at a range of audiences: students of finance and corporate trainers, business managers, corporate finance practitioners, investors, portfolio managers and security analysts. The third sentence of the first chapter of the book reads: 'Beneath the techniques and methods we present lies the belief that maximizing shareholder value is or ought to be the fundamental goal of all businesses.'[8] Acknowledging that 'maximizing shareholder value is often seen as shortsighted, inefficient, simplistic, and perhaps antisocial', they go on to explain why, on the basis of both theory and empirical evidence, they believe that these criticisms are mistaken.

Here is one way of summarizing some of the underlying theory.

- Shareholders, or investors, entrust corporate managers with their money. They want the managers to make them better off.
- Corporate managers should invest that money in projects whose likely financial returns are greater than the cost of the money which the investors supplied.
- The cost of that money is the opportunity cost of capital; that is, the financial return which the investors could have achieved on that money by investing it in something else.
- Financial returns are related to risk, and managers should take account of the risk associated with undertaking particular projects.
- Investors have access to borrowing and lending and to other investment opportunities, in the form of financial and stock markets. To protect the value of their assets they will diversify into a range of investments through such capital markets.
- Consequently, for investors, the risk profile for an individual investment is related to the correlation between the returns on that investment and the return on the market portfolio of investments.
- Corporate managers should therefore invest in projects whose risk-adjusted return is greater than the return on the market portfolio, and do not need to know anything about the individual circumstances of shareholders.
- Financial returns are measured in terms of cash flows, discounted at the applicable cost of capital, to obtain the net present value of the project.

This approach maximizes the financial returns to shareholders, and so maximizes their utility. It separates decisions about the timing of consumption from decisions about investment. It also enables the separation of ownership and control of companies.

The key assumptions required for this theory to work include that people always prefer more to less, and that borrowing and lending rates are similar. A further common assumption is that stock markets are, in the technical sense, efficient, at least to a fair degree. This modern corporate finance theory is based on financial economics, incorporating utility theory, portfolio theory, arbitrage pricing, market efficiency, option pricing theory and the capital asset pricing model. Like many other areas of study, financial economics and corporate finance theory has created its own sometimes esoteric world. Internally consistent and self-reinforcing, it can seem impenetrable to outsiders. Yet its conclusions permeate contemporary business thinking.

Despite some critiques and assaults, shareholder value rides high in financial academia. From there it has been widely translated into more popular management theories. One of these is 'value based management' (VBM). One of the world's leading accountancy and management consultancy firms, KPMG, produced a report entitled, 'Value based management: The growing importance of shareholder value in Europe'. In one of KPMG's own publications, they describe VBM as 'a management approach which puts shareholder value creation at the centre of the company philosophy. The maximization of shareholder value directs company strategy, structure and processes – it governs executive remuneration and dictates what measures are used to monitor performance.' In case that was not clear enough, 'VBM is about satisfying customer and employee needs to enhance shareholder value – not the other way round.'[9]

That final remark is significant. Anthony Hilton explained the shift:

> One of Britain's most successful fund managers remarked privately the other day that British executives no longer think that they are in business to make widgets, nor to ensure that their company is in a position to make widgets for years to come. Instead they now believe their prime purpose is to deliver enhanced value to shareholders, and they interpret this as having to deliver an ever-higher share price. This, he says, is a total change from 10 years ago.[10]

In the early 1980s, one of the most widely read management books was, *In Search of Excellence!*, by Peters and Waterman. In 1998, PricewaterhouseCoopers (then Price Waterhouse) published *In Search of Shareholder Value*, which has been translated into eight languages. John Coombe, the finance director of GlaxoWellcome, put it succinctly: 'Delivering shareholder value must be the ultimate objective of all management teams.'[11] There are both carrots and sticks which drive top managers to this approach. First we consider two sticks, and then turn to a particularly big and juicy carrot.

Corporate control

The shareholders of a company have the power to replace the management. They do not often use this power, but when they do it is usually the chief executive, often the finance director and sometimes the chairman who go. What shareholders more often do is to allow another company to take over the firm, and replace the management. Either way, some of the most senior people lose their jobs, and suffer the ignominy of being booted out, sometimes with little more than a year's remuneration as the pay-off to ease their indignity and tide them over. Since it is the shareholders who have this power, keeping your shareholders happy is a pretty good way to protect your job.

Some time ago, Marks & Spencer's shareholders were becoming restless at some of the company's difficulties. Part of the company's response was to place an advertisement for a 'Manager – Shareholder Value'. 'Marks & Spencer is changing,' the advert explained. A new programme designed for 'maximizing shareholder value' was under way, and it 'has already brought about profound transformation to Marks & Spencer'.[12] The market for corporate control is one in which shareholders rule. As more open approaches to company ownership extend, the pressure on managers to keep shareholders well rewarded increases. The threat of takeover is a crude mechanism, but an effective one.

Shareholder activism

A significant change over recent years is that the threat of takeover has become joined with the threat of direct action by shareholders. This was publicized for example by 'Calpers', the 'California Public Employees Retirement Scheme'. This huge pension fund started to target changes in underperforming companies in their investment portfolio. Notice that here is a body acting in the interests of public sector employees to demand greater focus on shareholder value.

Pension funds have become more focused on the performance their investment managers are achieving; they are replacing managers who fail to perform. This makes those managers focus on getting the investments they choose to make strong returns; so they pressurize corporate executives to deliver shareholder value. As benchmarks and index tracking become more pervasive, this trend will increase and intensify. Pressure will be transmitted from pension fund trustees through fund managers to company management. What they all want is shareholder value.

Enough of the sticks. What about the carrot?

Executive remuneration

Here, too, underlying theory has been introduced. Methodology comes in various forms, a popular one being economic value added (EVA), associated with Stern Stewart. This seeks to link executive reward directly to the value provided to shareholders. This principle has been explicitly promoted in recent years in corporate governance initiatives, such as the Greenbury Report, in the UK. Now it seems to me quite appropriate for the rewards which managers – and indeed all staff – receive to be linked to the interests of shareholders. I regard as one of our achievements when I was finance director of a quoted manufacturing plc, that about 70 per cent of the UK workforce were shareholders in the company.

This principle can extend rather further though: according to *Forbes* magazine, 800 of the top US chief executives between them hold stock in their companies with a value of more than $240 billion. That makes the mere $5 billion in remuneration which they received for 1998 – albeit much of it contingent on performance – seem rather paltry![13]

So the carrot for executives to pursue the interests of shareholders has both the technical design and structure, as well as the size and juiciness, to entice them. For them at least some of the effects are clear. What of the wider picture?

3. What effects does shareholder value have?

Globalization is associated with markets operating on a more integrated basis across the world. As financial markets do so, they drive global capital to seek ever more shareholder value; and as markets for goods and services become globalized, the drive for shareholder value leads companies to operate on a global basis in the way they relate to these markets. There are many ways in which shareholder value manifests itself.

Debates about the purpose of companies

A fundamental debate is between those who adopt the shareholder value approach, and those who subscribe to the wider stakeholder approach. In the latter, management have the task of promoting the business of a company, taking the interests of a wider group of stakeholders (such as investors, suppliers, customers and employees) into account. Such a view can provoke quite a response:

> The most ridiculous word you hear in boardrooms these days is 'stakeholders'. A stakeholder is anyone with a stake in a company's well-being. That includes its employees, suppliers, the communities in which it operates, and so on. The current theory is that a CEO has to take all these people into account in making decisions. Stakeholders! Whenever I hear that word, I ask 'How much did they pay for their stake?' Stakeholders don't pay for their stake. Shareholders do.[14]

This comes from Al Dunlap, author of *Mean Business*, and also known as 'Rambo in Pinstripes', and 'Chainsaw Al', for his approach to the management of companies.

A rather different approach was taken by the Royal Society of Arts when it launched some years ago an investigation into 'Tomorrow's Company'. The outcome was a vision of the 'inclusive approach' – a phrase which carefully sidestepped the use of the term 'stakeholder', but was essentially promoting a view which widened the duties of directors.

The Company Law Steering Group, set up by the UK government, published a framework document outlining the main issues.[15] The committee distinguished between several possible models. The first is 'enlightened shareholder value', in which maximizing shareholder value is to be done in a responsible way. This means recognizing the need for 'long term and trusting relationships with employees, suppliers, customers and others as appropriate in order to secure the success of the enterprise over time'. The second model is 'pluralism', in which responsibilities to those other than shareholders are explicitly recognized. A key distinction then comes in whether directors are *permitted* to consider these other interests, or are *required* to do so.

How this plays out in practice can be illustrated from ICI's statements of its objectives. In the mid-1980s, the company described its purpose as 'a responsible application of chemistry and related science. Through achievement of this aim we will serve our customers, employees and earn returns for our shareholders and the communities which we serve.' A decade later, it was 'to create shareholder value by focusing on businesses in which we have cost leadership, a price advantage and a market-leading position'. This last statement could probably be made by most companies – it says little about the firm, other than that it has adopted the shareholder value mantra.

Tension between means and ends

John Kay, a leading contemporary thinker on these matters, expresses it this way:

> The shareholder value approach is fundamentally instrumental: meeting customer needs is a means not an end. When the shareholder value maximizing firm expresses concern for the welfare of its employees, it does so not because it has genuine concern, and if its managers do they must try to suppress it; it does so because it fears that failure to express such concern would be bad for its long-term profitability . . . What is wrong with instrumental approaches to human relationships is not just that they are immoral. It is also that they rarely work for long. And mostly, we understand that . . . The essential point is not that profitable businesses are good businesses – they may or may not be – but that good businesses are profitable. And for the straightforward reason that being profitable is one of the things – although not the only thing – that good business is about. So stakeholding does not suggest corporate executives should attempt to advance the public interest. It simply claims that business has more than one responsibility and more than one measure of success.[16]

A contrary view has been expressed by Lucy Kellaway, also writing in the *Financial Times*:

> Companies exist to make money. They should be good to their employees because if they are not, no one will want to work for them. They should offer family friendly policies for exactly the same reason. That is to say, most employers have a *business* responsibility to ensure family life works. If they employ people with families, but do not recognize their needs, then their competitors will and they will lose out . . . Morality has nothing to do with it, and neither should it. The idea that our employers have a moral interest in us or our families is repugnant. We are grown-ups and we run our private lives as we see fit.[17]

So the question is, should companies take account of wider stakeholder interests if this does *not* lead to increased shareholder value? What happens if being 'good' actually reduces shareholder value? Some proponents of the stakeholder approach say that management should look beyond mere financial return. On the other hand, they are often all too quick to tell their opponents that companies which follow the practices which they advocate will also be more prosperous. This is rather like the old preacher who extolled the moral virtues of honesty, adding just before he left the pulpit that it also paid. When honesty pays, the decision is easy; the issue is what we do when it does not, or at least when it does not pay us. If we think that measuring the validity of a stakeholder approach can be done only by demonstrating that it offers superior shareholder value, then we may have capitulated over the fundamental issue. These matters become still more acute when we turn more explicitly to ethical questions.

The ethics of business

Adam Smith, often regarded as a founder of modern economics, understood that business and ethics must go together. He wrote *The Theory of Moral Sentiments* (1759) as well as his better known work, *The Wealth of Nations* (1776). Nearer to our own time, things may not be so clear. In June 1996, *International Risk Management* magazine ran on its front cover a full-colour picture of a child helping to build railways in Burma. The headline on the cover read, 'Is your responsibility to Shareholders or to this Child?' The article inside began: 'Risk management is not about protecting the ethical behaviour of a company. It is not about being a moral conscience. It is about protecting shareholders' assets.'[18]

The article focused on a pipeline being built by Total Oil at a cost of $1 billion to supply gas. The magazine pointed out that the United Nations Human Rights Commission had reported that 'torture, summary and arbitrary executions, forced labour, abuse to women, politically-motivated arrests and detention, forced displacement, important restrictions on the freedom of expression and association, and oppression of ethnic and religious minorities' routinely occur in Burma. Nevertheless, this was how the magazine summarized the approach to be taken to the decision as to whether Total should continue to operate in the country.

> Given the premise that the purpose of risk management is to protect shareholder value, the calculation for Total is a simple one. Compare the expected profit stream of the pipeline over its lifetime – which may or may not be shortened by conflict within the area – minus investment costs and other relevant financials, with the damage that continued involvement would incur.

This shareholder value approach to business ethics was set out more fully in a book by Elaine Sternberg called *Just Business*, in 1994.[19] Sternberg has two propositions: first, the sole task of business is to maximize the long-term value of the owners' stake by selling goods and services. It is not to exercise 'social responsibility'. She argues that the use of company resources for non-profitable but moral purposes is 'theft: an unjustified appropriation of the owners' property'. On the other hand, her second proposition is that everyone in business has a duty to behave ethically. This is defined to refer to the means used to achieve commercial objectives, and not to deviations from such objectives for supposedly worthwhile goals.

It is around ethical choices, around means and ends, that shareholder value and the stakeholder approach are critically distinguished.

Alienation

If you ask most people what their company makes, they might reply, 'consumer packaging', or 'car batteries'. If you ask a devotee of shareholder value what a company makes, the reply might be, 'Oh, about £20 million a year'. This distillation of everything into monetary values creates alienation between the articulated purpose and focus of a commercial activity, and the experience of most of those who work in and around it. Oxfam has attracted a number of applicants for senior positions who have been stimulated to leave their private-sector employers precisely when it was explained to them that their purpose and that of the firm was ultimately the creation of shareholder value. Not wanting to devote their working lives entirely to this, they decided to seek alternative employment.

On the other hand, I well remember an incident when I was a pension fund trustee. One of my fellow trustees was an employee representative, and an active trade unionist. At the pension meeting, he expressed to our fund manager the view that we should increase our investment in a particular company, as it had recently announced major restructuring plans which were likely to increase its profits considerably. I expressed some surprise at his view, pointing out that this restructuring would entail the loss of a large number of jobs, and suggested that if we as the management of the company for which he worked had announced something similar, he would in his trade union capacity have been objecting in the strongest possible terms. He acknowledged the distinction, and explained that it all depended on what perspective you had and what your interests were. The domination of economic life today by those whose sole purpose is to make money increases this alienation.

Traditionally, companies compete in a market for goods and services, and require capital to do so. The shareholder value model turns this upside down, so that companies compete in a market for capital, by providing attractive returns from the sale of goods and services. On the other hand, we should acknowledge that the shareholder value approach often means that chief executives are held responsible, and tend to feel accountable. A difficulty of the stakeholding model is that an executive who is theoretically responsible to everyone for everything is in practice not responsible to anyone for anything.

4. What might God make of shareholder value?

Although not expressed in such terms, some of Jesus' parables deal with business scenarios which might be recognized in a book of finance case-studies. The story of the shrewd manager in Luke 16 tells of a manager entrusted with the assets of an investor. Called to explain his poor investment performance, the manager distributes some of the investor's assets to his business associates, in the hope that they will befriend him when his appointment as fund manager is terminated early. This is a rather difficult story, but my point here is not the message that Jesus is teaching, but that he uses an economic story which is not so far removed from today.

What Jesus does do in that story is to distinguish between wealth and true riches. Remember, it is immediately following that parable that Luke records the famous words of Jesus, 'No one can serve two masters . . . You cannot serve both God and money' (Luke 16: 13). Shareholder value tends to adopt a limited view of humans. It is an inadequate and flawed view, in which we become 'economoids'. People are subjected to the 'nothing buttery' which regards them as nothing but economic beings. This may be clever thinking, but it is too self-contained. We need rather a 'joined up' approach, which takes account of the multiple aspects of created human identity.

5. How should we relate to shareholder value?

We first need to recognize those areas where we endorse, support or benefit from shareholder value. Most obviously this occurs when we have pension arrangements, insurance or many forms of savings. All these rely on the returns to shareholders, and so if we want to get the best pension for our money, the cheapest insurance on the market, the highest return on our savings, then we are expecting those to whom we entrust our money to create shareholder value with it. This can cause acute ethical dilemmas. A famous example is that of the Church Commissioners who managed the Church of England's £3 billion investment funds. In 1991, their QC argued in the High Court that they would be acting fecklessly if they followed strict Christian teaching on attitudes to wealth. He read extracts from the Sermon on the Mount, warning that one could not serve God and money. He argued that such Christian fecklessness might be a sign of outstanding sanctity in an individual, but that it was neither permissible nor admirable in those responsible for the pay, pensions and housing of present and future generations of Church of England clergy.

We participate in the world of globalization and shareholder value in our lives as customers and consumers. There has been publicity and criticism of highly paid chief executives whose bonuses have been raised in line with higher profits as a result of widespread redundancies. For example, Robert Allen, chief executive of AT&T, the telecommunications giant, was paid $3.4 million in the year that he announced 40,000 redundancies. What drives such downsizing decisions is the combined power of shareholders and consumers: shareholders, because they demand value; and consumers, because they too demand value. It has been argued that such chief executives are only responding to the orders of their masters – the consumers who buy their goods. If we were content to buy exactly the same goods from the same companies at the same prices year after year, then such jobs might be preserved. But we are not happy with the status quo. We want to buy new products, or the same products at lower prices, the latest and fastest gadget. If another supplier offers a better deal, we switch. But if we choose to behave in this fickle fashion, we should be careful about condemning corporate executives for taking the steps that are necessary to meet our demands. In this sense it is we, not they, who are demanding changes in the composition of the workforce, and implicitly saying that the skills of some of our fellows are now redundant.

This uncomfortable combination of our own power as consumers with the pressures for value to be returned to shareholders catches us all to a greater or lesser extent. And if we are tempted to react by becoming envious of those whom the prevailing system rewards very well, we should take care not to capitulate to the view that material rewards are the most important thing in life.

Yet we should be cautious of the views of those who try to divorce shareholder value from their own wealth. Military people will claim that the essence of their way of life consists of comradeship, physical activity, fitness and discipline – indeed, anything else but a refined capacity for death and destruction. In the same way, people who work in the City and in business would insist that their life revolves around professional expertise, the satisfaction of a job well done, co-operation with others, service to clients – anything indeed, apart from a refined capacity to make a lot of money. And as military people claim that only fully professional members can properly understand their ways, so also in business.

Conclusion

Shareholder value is an assumption underlying much of modern business thinking and practice. As an analytical tool, it can enable us to understand and predict, and be used in a 'positive' manner. As a guiding principle, when it is used in a 'normative' way, it can become much more sinister. Imagine it applied to the world of music.

The chief executive of a company was given a ticket for a performance of Schubert's Unfinished Symphony. Since she was unable to go, she gave the ticket to a friend who was an economist, and worked for a firm of management consultants. The next morning she asked him how he had enjoyed the performance. Instead of a few observations about the symphony in general, she was handed a formal memorandum which read as follows:

(1) For a considerable period, the oboe players had nothing to do. Their number should be reduced, and their work spread over the whole orchestra, avoiding peaks of inactivity.
(2) All twelve violins were playing identical notes. This seems an unneeded duplication, and the staff of this section should be cut. If a volume of sound is really required, this could be accomplished with the use of an amplifier.
(3) Much effort was involved in playing the semi-quavers. This appears to be an excessive refinement, and it is recommended that all shorter notes be rounded up to the nearest quaver. If this were done, it would be possible to use para-professionals instead of experienced musicians.
(4) No useful purpose is served by repeating with horns the passage that has already been handled by the strings. If all such redundant passages were eliminated, then the concert could be reduced from two hours to twenty minutes.
(5) The symphony had two movements. If Schubert did not achieve his musical goals by the end of the first movement, then he should have stopped there. The second movement is unnecessary and should be cut.
(6) In the light of the above, I can only conclude that had Schubert given attention to these matters, he would probably have had time to finish the symphony.

We should recognize our own participation in the world of shareholder value, as consumers, viewers and surfers; as current or future pensioners; as those who have insurance or savings. We may often have done well out of these, and probably hope that we will continue to do so.

So what *can* we do? We can ask challenging questions, and change the framework in which the discussion takes place. In the field of education, a good educational institution will see its efforts translated into strong exam results; but strong exam results in themselves do not equate to good education. Likewise in business with regard to profits: a good company will achieve strong profitability; but strong profitability does not equate to a good company. What does that perspective say about shareholder value?

We can also do fascinating things, reflecting the nature of *The God of Surprises*.[20] The Rich Young Ruler who met Jesus went away sad at the challenge to liquidate his assets and distribute the proceeds to the poor (Luke 18: 18–25). But Tom Monaghan, the founder of Domino's Pizza, influenced by C. S. Lewis's book *Mere Christianity*,[21] decided in 1998 to sell and give away most of his $1 billion stake in the company, together with his helicopter, yacht, aircraft and private island, dismissing them all as 'distractions'. You and I probably have rather less scope to hit the headlines in quite that way – but we can all make surprising choices, the explanation to which beckons to a greater reality than the narrower world of global shareholder value.

In his book, *Competing for the Future*, the strategy consultant and academic Gary Hamel asked, 'Among the people who work on strategy in organizations and the theorists, a huge proportion, perhaps 95%, are economists and engineers who share a mechanistic view of strategy. Where are the theologists, the anthropologists to give broader and fresher insights?'[22] As one of the 5 per cent minority, I hope that I may have demonstrated that some theologians may indeed have some broader and fresher insights to bring.

Notes

1 Francis Fukuyama, *Trust: The Social Virtues and the Creation of Prosperity* (London, 1995).

2 George Soros, *The Crisis of Global Capitalism* (Boston, MA, 1998).
3 Reinhold Niebuhr, *Moral Man and Immoral Society* (New York, 1941), 177.
4 A. Clements, in 'Mastering management', supplement to the *Financial Times* (31 May 1996).
5 Milton Friedman, *Capitalism and Freedom* (Chicago, 1962), 133.
6 James P. Walsh, in 'Mastering strategy', supplement to the *Financial Times* (8 November 1999).
7 R. A. Brealey and S. C. Myers, *Principles of Corporate Finance*, 4th edn (New York, 1991).
8 Thomas E. Copeland, Tim Koller and Jack Murrin, *Valuation: Measuring and Managing the Value of Companies*, 2nd edn (New York, 1996), 3.
9 *Consulting Matters*, 23 (Summer 1999, KPMG Consulting).
10 A. Hilton, 'Weighing up the fat cats', *Management Today* (July 1999, 47).
11 A. Black, P. Wright and J. E. Bachman, *In Search of Shareholder Value: Managing the Drivers of Performance* (London, 1998).
12 Advertisement in *Financial Times* (16 September 1999).
13 Cited by Walsh, 'Mastering strategy'.
14 Al Dunlap, cited by J. Kay, 'Ethics and the role of business in society', *RSA Journal*, 3/4 (1999), 77.
15 The Company Law Steering Group, Department of Trade and Industry, *Modern Company Law for a Competitive Economy: Company Formation and Capital Maintenance: A Consultation Document* (London, 1999).
16 John Kay, 'The root of the matter', *Financial Times* (10 February, 1999).
17 Lucy Kellaway, 'Steer clear of the morality minefield', *Financial Times* (25 May 1998).
18 M. Hanley, 'Ethics and business: bedfellows for the '90s?', *International Risk Management* (June 1996).
19 Elaine Sternberg, *Just Business* (Boston, MA, 1994), 41.
20 Gerard Hughes, *The God of Surprises* (London, 1985).
21 C. S. Lewis, *Mere Christianity* (London, 1952).
22 Gary Hamel, interview in the *Financial Times* (3 May 1996).

4

Co-operatives: regenerating business in the twenty-first century

ROGER SAWTELL

On a world scale we live in a wealthy society and are often told by politicians and advertising people that an even wealthier society will make us happier and better. They say that shiny cars will bring a sense of fulfilment and wall-to-wall carpets will bring ease of mind. However, the evidence does not support the politicians nor the advertisers who, of course, have their own axes to grind. The road to fulfilment lies in a quite different direction. It is to do with the spiritual journey and it is to do with relationships and with justice.

This leads us to study the structure of the organizations in which we work because work is a dominant part of our lives. The challenge for the new century is to adopt structures which enable more people to find abundant enjoyment and fulfilment in their work. The thesis of this chapter is that the employee-owned co-operative enterprise is the most promising structure for industry and commerce in the twenty-first century. Most promising, that is, for those concerned with quality of life at work rather than merely maximizing the return on capital. Promising for those concerned with justice rather than perpetuating the historical master/servant relationship. Quality and justice are concepts firmly rooted in the Old and New Testaments, but they are equally important to many who do not regard themselves as practising Christians.

The chapter is not specifically about the financial viability of enterprises, but it is taken as read that survival in the market economy, in which we are placed, is just as important for a co-operative as for any other business. If the enterprise is not sustainable, it disappears and its concerns for quality of life at work and for justice disappear with it.

What distinguishes a co-operative from a conventional company

An employee-owned co-operative is a business owned and democratically controlled by the people working in it. Historically, this structure has been variously called a producer co-operative or a worker co-operative or an industrial co-operative, to distinguish it from the high street shops which are retail co-operatives owned by the customers. In the employee-owned co-operative, if the assets are collectively owned by members by virtue of working in the business, it may also be called a 'common ownership'. Co-operative shares in a registered co-operative society do not carry votes in proportion to shares held, nor do they vary in value; they are, effectively, loans and quite different from equity shares. A single share in a co-operative is often considered as a 'membership ticket' and has little or no intrinsic monetary value. One-person-one-vote is a fundamental co-operative principle,[1] whereas in an equity share company votes are in proportion to shares, so that the holder of 50 per cent of the shares controls the company.

A share company incorporated under the Companies Act is legally enabled to adopt a wide spectrum of objects, but seldom does so. Usually the accepted object is entirely financial, to optimize the gain for shareholders by means of dividends or capital appreciation, the so-called 'bottom line'. For example, referring to the concept of limited liability whereby a limited company cannot be held responsible for its debts, the historian Arthur Bryant wrote:

> The consequences of the Companies Act of 1862 were perhaps greater than that of any single measure in English Parliamentary history. They completed the divorce between the Christian conscience and the economic practice of everyday life. They paganized the commercial community. Henceforward, an astute man by adherence to legal rules which had nothing to do with morality could grow immensely rich by virtue of shuffling off his most elementary obligations to his fellows. He could not only grow rich by such means, he could grow immensely powerful.[2]

By contrast, a co-operative society registered under the Industrial and Provident Societies Act cannot have 'the object of making profits mainly for the payment of interest, dividends',[3] and will therefore adopt objects which are to do with the seven co-operative principles: open membership, democratic control, use of surplus, autonomy, provision of education, mutual help between co-operatives, concern for the community.

For example, the ICOM Model Rules, first written in 1976 and used in one form or another by hundreds of employee-owned co-operatives, state: 'The co-operative shall have regard to promoting the physical, mental and spiritual well-being of . . . those who participate in the activities of the co-operative by reason of employment . . . and to assist people in need by any means whatsoever.'[4] This objects clause contrasts with the capital-ownership ethos typified by Henry Ford who said 'Why is it I get a whole person when all I want is a pair of hands?' This is the heart of the difference between capital-ownership and employee-ownership. A co-operative is a participative business, not solely as a means of increasing its productivity but because its legal structure compels participation. It is holistic. This participation is much more than that of a company with an employee share scheme in which the majority of shares are carefully retained by the outside shareholders who remain the capital owners.

Under the principle of open membership, all permanent employees of a co-operative are entitled to be voting members, subject to qualifying age and service, so there is universal suffrage. In national politics in Britain and USA the two principles of one-person-one-vote and universal suffrage have been accepted for many years[5] as they have been also in the administration of the local tennis club or other voluntary committee. Therefore, it is strange that in industry and commerce which take up such a dominant proportion of the time and energy of most people, neither universal suffrage nor one-person-one-vote have made much headway. Why not? There are a number of historical and cultural reasons, but the chief one is that the capital providers, the large shareholders and City institutions, have been able to smother and extinguish changes which would limit their power. In an age of universal education, this has been an extraordinary feat, achieved mainly by playing upon the greed of small investors. In effect, the capital owner says,

> Allow me to control the company and I will ensure you are paid a good dividend on your minority share. Because I am a professional, it will be a larger dividend than could be achieved if you took an active part in

> the decision-making process. I am a business person, bound by the Companies Act, so do not ask me irrelevant questions about social justice.

This capital-ownership control has succeeded in making Britain a rich country by world standards, but we hardly notice that most of us working in commerce or industry have little or no voice in the organization to which we give our time and talents. Like Esau, we have parted with our rights for a bowl of soup.[6] Very tasty soup and a large bowl but, nevertheless, it is only a bowl of soup. And we barely notice the poverty of most of the Third World.

Some employee-ownership events of the nineteenth century

By 1800 there were 500 Watt's steam engines in action and each one made it possible to employ large numbers of workers under one factory roof. Craft workshops were giving way to mechanized cotton mills, steelworks and coalmines. The industrial revolution, which was to change the world by the end of the century, was gathering momentum. Adam Smith, a lecturer in Moral Philosophy at Glasgow University, before there was any such occupation as an economist, developed the philosophy of the free-market economy. The initial benefits would accrue to the factory owner who had provided the capital to build the factory and buy the monster steam engine, but exploitation of his employees might be avoided, Smith thought, because the 'hidden hand' of the market might prevent monopoly power. The factory owners gleefully grasped this tentative idea because it appeared to give moral legitimacy to their new-found source of wealth. All they were called upon to do was to look after their own material interests and, by a process of economic osmosis, justice would trickle down to the poor. So that was all right. However, the truth was that Adam Smith had not only forecast the market economy but also perceived its moral dangers. 'But for what purpose is all the toil and bustle of this world?', he asked, and answered that it was for the welfare of the common man.[7] Therefore he advocated public expenditure on universal education to raise awareness and participation. He was frequently hostile to the grasping motives of businessmen and was, in fact, an early champion of the consumer.

It was convenient for the factory owners to ignore this latter part of his teaching.

There were others, too, who were concerned about the social consequences of rapid industrialization and the formal co-operative movement, initiated by the Rochdale Pioneers in 1844, developed steadily during these mid-century years. There was an upsurge of employee-owned co-operatives started by a remarkable group who called themselves Christian Socialists and came together 'to pioneer the way to a new and better social order', in contrast to the owners of capital. They stood for 'a living community under Christ . . . in which there is spiritual fellowship and practical co-operation'.[8] This group included public figures such as F. D. Maurice, Professor of Theology at King's College, London, and Charles Kingsley, who wrote *The Water Babies*.[9] They supported producer co-operatives in trades such as tailoring, printing and shoe-making, but most of them foundered when the co-operative movement threw its weight behind the development of customer-owned business, the high street co-op shops, to the exclusion of employee-ownership. It was an idea before its time. (It compares with Tony Benn's courageous but unsuccessful attempt to give government backing in the 1970s to Triumph motorbikes, a failing capital-owned company, to re-form as an employee-owned co-operative. The management experience needed to sustain a medium-sized co-operative business was not yet in place.)

Meanwhile, in the nineteenth century, the owners of capital were busy consolidating their gains and shuffling off their 'most elementary obligations' to their fellows. They grew rich and powerful and were pleased to claim Adam Smith as their own philosopher/economist, studiously ignoring his concern for wider educational opportunities for the labouring poor. They worked diligently to achieve monopolies by price-fixing with their competitors or buying them out and closing them down. *Laissez-faire* capital-ownership developed steadily for the remainder of the century and its influence gradually reached out to all corners of the world in search of raw materials and markets. The multinational company was in the making, bringing substantial increases to the material standard of living in the West, but endemic and desperate poverty to millions in developing countries.

Some employee-ownership events of the twentieth century

Heavily influenced by the socialist writers Beatrice and Sidney Webb, the emerging Labour Party in the early part of the twentieth century chose 'public ownership', otherwise called nationalization, rather than employee-ownership, as the preferred alternative to capital-ownership. The Webbs argued that working men were incapable of efficient administration. Maybe they had a case, and further education, as proposed by Adam Smith a century earlier, was needed before employee-owned enterprises could be sustained. But their word was so influential that there was little experimentation and the cause of employee-owned co-operatives was set back by fifty years. The handful of producer co-operatives carried over from the Victorian era limped along, diminished by occasional closures and not augmented by new initiatives. There was a transitory revival in the 1920s, called Guild Socialism, but it received little support from the Labour Party and faded away. Meanwhile the Co-operative movement was concentrating on retail co-operatives, the high street shops with the 'divi', with conspicuous success. Membership grew steadily, reaching 11 million by mid-century,[10] so that half the adult population were active Co-op shoppers and millions could quote their Co-op number as easily as their birth date.

It was not until the 1960s that there was any significant revival of employee-ownership, and it came from the flower-power, make-love-not-war culture which attracted huge numbers of young people at that time. In due course the hippies needed to earn a living, as well as going to rock music festivals, and what was more appropriate than a mutual love-your-neighbour co-operative business? Co-ops sprang up like magic mushrooms in a meadow and more were formed in the 1970s than in the whole of the previous fifty years. Some called themselves 'common ownerships', others preferred 'worker co-operatives' with its overtones of solidarity with the workers. This was rather strange as most of these new 'workers' were flower-people who were far removed from those earnest Victorian co-operators dedicated to the Protestant work ethic.

One of the very few established employee-owned businesses at that time was Scott Bader, a successful medium-sized chemical manufacturer developed by a Quaker, Ernest Bader, who had transferred the ownership to his employees in 1951. At their works at Wollaston, deep in the Northamptonshire countryside, on 12 June 1971, the Industrial Common Ownership Movement (ICOM)[11] was born and gradually became accepted as the national body of employee-owned businesses. These new enterprises were mostly in labour-intensive trades like publishing, building, printing and hardly realized that they were re-inventing the producer co-operatives pioneered by the Christian Socialists a hundred years earlier. So for twenty years, until the 1990s, ICOM developed independently of the wider Co-operative movement which showed surprisingly little interest in employee-ownership.

Each of these new businesses needed a legal constitution and ICOM soon realized that the Industrial and Provident Societies Act, under which co-operatives of all kinds had been registered for over a century, provided an appropriate structure. The problem was that the traditional rules, to comply with the Act, had been augmented but not revised since Victorian times and now ran to a hundred pages, many of them incomprehensible in the 1970s and quite unnecessarily complex. So ICOM in 1975 published a revised version of Model Rules[12] 'on one page of A3' and subsequently several further sets of updated Rules for different types of co-operative businesses. Hundreds of newly formed employee-owned enterprises joined ICOM and used these Model Rules to achieve a simple one-person-one-vote constitution, without needing to employ solicitors, most of whom knew little of co-operatives and charged outrageous fees to prepare inappropriate incorporated company constitutions which they had readily at hand from their work with conventional companies.

These ICOM co-operative entrepreneurs, wise as serpents if not gentle as doves, had taken note of the danger of a successful co-operative coming under pressure to dissolve or sell the business, and divide the spoils amongst themselves, despite the fact that a large part of these spoils had been earned by the work and thrift of their predecessor employee-members who had retained funds in the common pot to strengthen the business and enable it to survive hard times. Therefore the ICOM Model Rules of 1975, and subsequent revisions in 1977 and 1980, all included a dissolution clause under which residual assets cannot be paid out to members but must be transferred to another co-operative organization with similar objects. Under these rules there is no financial incentive to sell out and every encouragement to keep the business going, continue to provide a livelihood for the members and retain the social objects of the co-operative. If building societies and mutual insurance companies had had a similar entrenched dissolution clause, the demutualizations of the 1980s and 1990s might not have been possible without an Act of Parliament. The carpet-baggers, who joined just to encourage the mutuals to sell out, would not have been able to steal the assets earned by former members.

However, there was another legal snag. Many new businesses start cautiously with only two or three employees and the Industrial and Provident Societies Act at that time specified a minimum of seven members. One of the pioneering co-ops, Daily Bread Co-operative, the first business to adopt the ICOM Model Rules, in 1976 circumnavigated this restriction by inviting into founder-membership a few people who were not employed in the business but were sympathetic supporters and advisers. The understanding was that they would resign when there were seven or more employee-members to satisfy the Act, and so they did. Bearing in mind that only two out of five new businesses survive the first two critical years, these outside people played a valuable supporting role, affirming and underpinning the tiny working group. Subsequently, some remained involved as 'wise-persons', but the decision-making group at Daily Bread Co-operative since 1984 has been composed entirely of employee-members.[13]

Other incipient co-operators at this time were not prepared to risk this compromise solution because they were not convinced that the 'outside' members would resign when the business grew and prospered. They also noted that some of the few remaining Victorian producer co-ops had passed out of the hands of current employees because they had allowed former employees to bequeath their voting shares to relatives, not working in the co-op, who had a diminishing concern for the social objects.[14] So, ICOM, with some moral hesitation, in 1980 devised an employee-owned form of Company Limited by Guarantee under the Companies Act, which required only two members and was therefore suitable for new businesses. Many employee-owned businesses were thus incorporated as companies in the 1980s rather than as registered co-operative societies. The co-operative principle of employee-membership was achieved but there was a price to pay because companies can be bought and sold more easily than registered societies. This did not escape the notice of sharp-eyed capital owners and disenchanted relatives of the founder-members, who saw it as a means of subverting the co-operative principles when the business was well-established and beyond the early high-risk years. What better than to let the employee-members carry the risk burden of the early years and then pounce on them when the business was moving into profit? Sadly, a handful of prosperous co-operatives did revert to capital-ownership, which would not have been possible if they had had the co-operative dissolution clause.

The new-start dilemma was resolved in 1996 when the Industrial and Provident Societies Act was amended[15] to allow a minimum of three members. Hopefuly this will encourage future employee-owned businesses to become part of the Co-operative movement as registered societies. Moreover, by using Model Rules the cost of initiating the business is minimized and protection is given against encroachment by unwanted predators or greedy disenchanted employee-members.[16]

From a base of about twenty employee-owned businesses when ICOM started in 1971, the total by 1980 had grown to 350 and by 1992 1,169 were listed.[17] During this almost unpublicized but historically significant growth phase of employee-ownership, the capital owners had not been idle and the multinationals made profitable use of new technology. The whole century has been one of growth, refinement and consolidation for capital owners. Companies combined to achieve what they claimed would be economies of scale but which were more often than not excuses to achieve monopoly. By the end of the century, a handful of multi-national companies spanned the world and challenged the power of governments in developing countries. Astute entrepreneurs, like Bill Gates at Microsoft and Rupert Murdoch in newspapers and television, not only built up huge fortunes but also gained immense and seemingly unaccountable power over their employees and local communities, scattered all around the world. Developing countries gained little and the provision of food, shelter and peaceful coexistence in many African countries was scarcer in the 1990s than it had been thirty years previously. Bill

Gates's assets of US $53 billion[18] were sufficient for him to feed the whole of the African continent, if he chose to do so.[19]

During the blizzard of ideas and activity in Victorian times, where this story began, John Stuart Mill, philosopher and economist had written in 1869: 'The emancipation of women and co-operative production are the two great changes which will regenerate society.'[20] More than 130 years later the first of Mill's predictions has happened and women are emancipated to a degree unimaginable in 1869, but 'co-operative production' has languished. Note that Mill, in his precise way, did not write of co-operative retailing, which did flourish, but co-operative production. His two predictions are linked because women are more natural co-operators than men. They strive less for power and they know the value of mutual encouragement. So the fact that women are now more acceptable and more commonplace as managers and entrepreneurs is one of the signs that the co-operative ethic, as opposed to the capital-ownership ethic, will become more widespread in the next century. This could be stated more specifically: co-operative production will only become commonplace when there are as many women as men in positions requiring leadership.

So, at the close of the twentieth century, employee-ownership is a marginal but healthy segment. It has not failed. It has not been tried on a significant scale, but it is now waiting in the wings, rejecting the parts which are no longer relevant and refining the parts which capital-ownership cannot reach. Most of industry and commerce remains in the hands of the capital owners. Remote bankers are morally silent or idealistically bankrupt, but they provide luxury food and foreign holidays, the contemporary equivalents of bread and circuses. What of the future? The prophecy is that Mill's second prediction will come to pass in the twenty-first century. Where is the evidence?

An example of employee-ownership, Daily Bread Co-operative

Daily Bread Co-operative was registered as an employee-owned co-operative society on 3 March 1976, the first to use the ICOM Model Rules. Market research and finding a suitable building with a long lease proceeded slowly and trading began on 1 October

1980 with a working group of three people. The work decided upon was preparing, packing and retail-selling of a range of wholefoods, defined as foods which had been processed as little as possible. This food includes grains, dried fruit, beans, nuts, herbs and spices, much of it organically grown and coming from all parts of the world. Nineteen years later, the working group is twenty people and sales are approaching £1 million. There are no outstanding loans and the balance sheet is strong, showing a ratio of current assets to current liabilities of 3.5 compared to an industry average of less than 2.

On one level it is a small well-established business with a reputation for friendly service and value for money. On another level it is unusual because it was not the brainchild of a conventional entrepreneur but grew out of a house group attached to a local church. As the business was to have a number of fundamental social objects, over and above the object of being sustainable in the market economy (see Table 4.1), and because employee-ownership is an area with few signposts, the founder members agreed that the working members should be Christians from various denominations. It was to be a response to the gospel taught by Jesus Christ, a way of life as well as a set of beliefs, a 'Monday church'. It was intended to be more 'light' than 'salt', a 'city built on a hill'[21] which cannot be hidden. There is a half-hour meeting for worship, Bible study and prayer, every morning during working time, led by members on a rota basis.[22] This is an integral part of the day's work and follows the Benedictine tradition that the prayer is the 'work of the community', just as much as the production of food or hospitality to visitors. The name was chosen with this concept in mind and it is not unusual for decisions about the business to be discerned from members praying together daily.

One social object is that there should be a number of people recovering from mental illness as part of the working group. Some have moved on to other work after recovery, others have become employee-members. Another ongoing concern is fair trading with suppliers from the Third World where much of the food originates. Over nineteen years, more than £100,000 has been donated to good causes from the annual surplus.

Salaries are modest and the same for all, with no differentials for responsibility or length of service or mental health as opposed

Table 4.1 Daily Bread Co-operative, Northampton: summary of audited accounts, 1990–1998

Yr ended 30 Sept.	*1990*	*1991*	*1992*	*1993*	*1994*	*1995*	*1996*	*1997*	*1998*
No. of people at year end (full-time equivalent)	20	20	19	19	18	17	18	16	16
Net sales (£000)	724	765	784	785	770	750	814	814	822
Gross profit, % of net sales	30	30	31	29	30	31	29	31	31
Net profit before tax (£000)	19	2	9	–7	1	8	–3	6	10
Donations to Third World community projects (£000)	8	2	12	8	10	7	7	7	8**
Loans outstanding (£000)	4	3	22*	21	15	11	6	4	0*
Current ratio (current assets divided by current liabilities)	2.4	2.1	1.5	1.5	2.0	2.1	2.2	2.6	3.5

* In 1992 £50,000 was spent on extra production space and equipment. These loans were repaid by the end of 1998.
** By September 1998 the cumulative donations to Third World and community projects exceeded £100,000.
General note: These are the accounts of Daily Bread Co-operative Ltd, Registered Society no. 21612R, Northampton NN4 7AD (tel. 01604 621531). Daily Bread Co-operative (Cambridge) opened on 1 December 1992, as a similar wholefood warehouse. Like Daily Bread, Northampton, it is an independent co-operative business, owned and controlled by the people working in it.

to mental disability. Allowances are paid for dependants such as children or grandparents, and there is an annual procedure for discussing the financial needs of each member. None are rich, none are in need and there is a high level of job security.[23] Trading in the market economy of the 1980s, an era when individualism was the politically correct stance, the equal salary policy at Daily Bread was unusual and radical, but seldom controversial among members. It has limited candidates available when a new manager is to be appointed, but it has also been a strength rather than a weakness in the development of the business because it ensures considerable flexibility.

The manager, appointed by those he or she is entrusted to manage, is given freedom to get on with the work, including critical buying decisions which, in the food business, cannot be delayed. On the other hand, people decisions are invariably referred to the weekly meeting. Daily Bread has developed a simple management pattern in a complex world and this simplicity has been a key to viability in the market-place. The constitutional rules are on a single sheet of paper and have not been altered in any way since 1976.

Growth for its own sake has never been an objective. The business needed to be viable and this required a turnover of £0.5 million in the 1980s, which was reached in six years without any expenditure on advertising. If the venture was worthwhile, the word would be passed on from one customer to another. But the enterprise also needed to be small enough for all the employee-owners to meet in one room for an hour each week to take decisions. A single-tier structure is easily understood but limits the working group to about twenty people.

Democratically controlled co-operatives do not have subsidiaries, by conviction, because the word 'subsidiary' denotes a different grade of employee. Bees, those social insects, do not have subsidiary hives; they start up a new independent but closely linked hive. So growth is organic and horizontal by means of other co-operatives starting up or hiving off. Daily Bread, Northampton, has helped a number of other employee-owned co-operatives, by making soft loans, taking on potential working members for training, advising on structures and by affirmation that this kind of enterprise is not commercial madness. For example, Daily Bread Co-operative (Cambridge) was initiated in

1992 by a group convened by a former manager from Northampton. By 1999 it had reached a turnover of £0.5 million and a working group of about twelve people.

Larger co-operatives struggle with a complex array of representatives and interlocking committees, but no clear-cut effective structure has yet emerged for twentieth-century medium or large employee-owned enterprises. It is similar to the run-up to Rochdale in 1844 and there is little doubt that viable appropriate co-operative structures will emerge during the twenty-first century. Two swallows do not make a summer and these two examples of small employee-owned co-operative businesses do not make an industrial revolution. But two experienced swallows attract others to sit alongside them on the phone wires. So two co-operatives which are proven rather than experimental, hammered out and refined over nineteen years in the fire of an unrelenting market economy, may attract others to follow in the new century. If not employee-ownership, what are the alternatives?

State-ownership as an alternative to capital ownership

The most widely disseminated alternative to capital-ownership during the twentieth century has not been employee-ownership but state-ownership, via communism or socialism. As far back as 1844, Engels published 'the most terrible verdict ever passed on the world of industrial slums'.[24] His response, in conjunction with Marx, was *The Communist Manifesto*, published in 1848. It was to be a further seventy years before any state of significance tried to put the manifesto into practice when the USSR was initiated in 1922. By this time both Marx and Engels had been dead for twenty-five years.[25]

However, state-ownership of industry and agriculture in Russia did not produce the classless just society which Marx and Engels had envisaged but, instead, the tyranny of Stalin, the inefficiency of collective farms and centrally controlled industry. The bureaucrats had their dachas by the lakeside but the poor remained unreasonably poor compared with the West. So, after political upheavals in the 1980s, state control of industry effectively collapsed in 1991 and subsequently fell into disuse in numerous other countries: clogs to clogs, as it were, in only two generations. By the end of the 1990s, apart from the mishmash of China, the only avowedly communist state of any size is North Korea, with a population of 22 million, many on the verge of starvation.

In Britain, state-ownership of the 'commanding heights of the economy' such as coal and steel between 1945 and 1980 was not considered a great success and suffered from too much bureaucracy and too little enterprise. Capital-ownership was reinstated in the 1980s and Prime Minister Thatcher declared that 'there was no alternative'. But Marx, 150 years after the *Manifesto*, was not to be outdone. He had argued that capitalism would destroy itself because the concept of unlimited private property would not be acceptable to an increasingly educated workforce running increasingly technical industrial processes. He forecast that it would breed its own successor, socialism, not the same as communism. 'What the bourgeois therefore produces', he wrote morbidly, 'are its own gravediggers.'[26] Perhaps he will yet be proved correct because the justice of this new wave of capital-ownership in the 1990s is now questioned as never before. Enormously wealthy capitalists are not seen as appropriate people to have so much power over the cultural and economic development of the world. Educated people with access to huge stores of information may accept that the likes of Murdoch and Gates are entitled to be millionaires and live in style as a reward for their entrepreneurial skills, but they are not justified in being powerful multi-billionaires, accountable to no one. There must be better qualifications than money for those in a position to change the world.

But, again, far-seeing Marx never claimed that state-ownership was the abiding answer. He said that economics would always be in a state of flux and that this dialectical, changeful, aspect would lead towards more people being involved in the decision-making process. He used words like proletariat, while we talk about informed employees with access to the internet. If Marx were writing today, it is possible he would see the dialectic leading not to the aridity of state-ownership as in communism, but to the broader more life-enhancing concept of employee-ownership, mutual control of the enterprise by those most closely associated with its objects. This is still socialist democracy, which he envisaged, but a quite different form from materialist communism. So Marx may be recruited as a prophet of the co-operative movement for the twenty-first century and there we must leave him!

Evidence for a change of economic culture

Short-term thinking may indicate that the British economy is in an irreversible situation. We are deeply, deeply, deeply dominated by material values and enslaved to economics and economists. J. M. Keynes said that economics should be 'a modest occupation similar to dentistry', but we have elevated economists to be immodest demi-gods. The *laissez-faire* scenario is that we will become even greedier, the rich capital-owners will become richer and the poor in the Third World will starve more frequently. Like Esau, we will forego our heritage in order to get a short-term slice of this wealth. Bill Gates will buy twenty million votes and become king of Britain.

However, there is another scenario, less obvious but more hopeful for those concerned with quality of life. Maybe we are reaching rock-bottom in this enslavement to possessions with its diminishing returns of fulfilment. Maybe the next century will witness an ascent from this trough, a renaissance of values other than the economic ones. What is the evidence which points in this direction with regard to employment?

Businesses with social objects

Employee-owned businesses have social objects as well as financial ones and there are more such businesses trading in 1999 than at any previous time since the industrial revolution. A few are large enterprises such as John Lewis Partnership with 40,000 employee-partners, others are medium-sized like Scott Bader with 450 people and the Baxi Partnership, making central heating boilers, with 970 people. But most of the listed 1,115 employee-owned enterprises[27] are small and therefore receive very little publicity.

Small is beautiful and coming soon

Electronic technology enables many work tasks to be achieved with smaller numbers of people. The age of the huge workforce under one roof is over because it is easier to hive off or sub-contract parts of the production task. The shift towards smallness, heralded by E. F. Schumacher in the 1970s,[28] is gathering momentum and makes employee-ownership a more viable option. Smallness also has the backing of the people. A MORI poll, conducted regularly since 1970, asks people if they agree that substantial profits for large British companies are 'a good thing'. In 1970 53 per cent said yes but by 1988 only 25 per cent were in favour. There is a growing distaste for the remote decision-making and lack of accountability of multinationals. Big industry will not go away in a hurry and the big will continue to merge and get bigger, but there will also be more opportunities for small value-based enterprises. Schumacher, an adviser to Scott Bader and a prophet in his own time, taught that nothing of consequence is changed until ownership is changed. Correspondingly, when the change to co-operative ownership occurs, then there is a significant cultural change. For example, during a recession, knowing that they may be made redundant at any time, employees in conventional capital-companies are unlikely to tighten their belts indefinitely to keep their remote employer out of bankruptcy. But if the employee is also the employer, as in a co-operative, the cultural situation is quite different. In the recessive period 1988–92, when most conventional companies were shedding labour, employee-owned co-operatives actually increased the number of people employed by 27 per cent.

Loan finance

Co-operatives raise their working capital by loans rather than by equity shares, and the Co-operative Bank, one of the liveliest of the second-line banks, with a strong ethical investment stance, has had an intrinsic concern for co-operative development for the past hundred years. Other relevant financial institutions are now emerging, such as Triodos Bank, which rejects the conventional wisdom that a bank's principal task is to maximize its financial performance. Triodos defines its purpose as financing 'projects and businesses working actively with social . . . issues', such as co-operatives. Lending grew by 64 per cent in 1997 and total funds reached £200 million.[29] The Ecology Building Society, founded in 1981, lends in support of 'earth-friendly lifestyles and businesses, such as co-operative living'. This is a small society, committed to mutuality, and the assets increased by 10 per cent in 1998 to £25 million.[30]

Industrial Common Ownership Finance

ICOF was initiated in 1973 as a revolving loan fund to assist the development of employee-ownership. It has grown slowly and steadily over twenty-five years and 1998 was the busiest year on record, with lending at £0.5 million and net assets of over £2 million. Losses were at an all-time low of 3.2 per cent,[31] a figure which would be the envy of most conventional lenders, who know that new businesses are bound to be a high risk.

Ethical investment

EIRIS, the Ethical Investment Research and Information Service, indicates that this is one of the fastest growing sectors in financial services. By 1988, 312,000 people had invested a total of more than £2 billion in unit and investment trusts concerned with ethical criteria. In the year to June 1998, the invested funds increased by nearly 50 per cent.[32] KPMG, one of the world's five largest firms of auditors, has initiated an ethical auditing service to help companies comply with non-financial targets.

Taken separately, these indicators are small when set alongside the capital-ownership structure with which we are familiar. But taken together they are evidence that fundamental changes are taking place within the culture of economics in Britain. The picture will look very different in a hundred years' time.

Servant leadership is the key

It may appear that the citadel of capital-ownership, with its walls, watchtowers and palaces, built, rebuilt and refined over two centuries, is impregnable. It may seem that the capital-owners have learnt to change with changing circumstances and bend with the remover to remove. But when we look at history with a long lens, as this chapter attempts to do, we see that no man-made institution is secure. The Roman Empire must have seemed impregnable but it declined and fell; the Roman Catholic Church dominated the Christian world for a thousand years until it began to decline in the seventeenth century; materialist communist state control captured half the world but then declined to almost nothing within two generations, in the twentieth century. So it is not unreasonable to predict that capital-ownership is no exception and will wither away and be absorbed by history when a sufficient number of people lose confidence in its capability to produce a more acceptable society.

The vision is that work is to be much more than earning a material living. It is to be for fulfilment and an abundance of joy. Men and women are not to be chained like dogs to the organization which provides their living, but are to be part of a working community which provides fellowship and friendship as well as bread: a holistic concept. The key is servant-leadership, the concept that the leader is 'servant first'[33] and business administrator second. The prophet Isaiah describes the servant-leader who will not break the bruised reed nor quench the dimly burning wick but will 'faithfully bring forth justice'.[34] The prophecy of the suffering servant was then borne out 800 years later by Jesus[35] whose leadership style was not to start by building a large organization but to spend a great deal of time talking and teaching with a small group of disciples. Just as the Christian Socialists were the initiators of the early wave of producer co-operatives in the nineteenth century, so will Christians in the twenty-first century be at the forefront of employee-ownership, talking, writing and, above all, doing the imperatives of the gospel of social justice and quality of life in the workplace.

We can learn from organizations which have a much longer history than industry. For example, Benedict founded a monastery, a working community, in about AD 540 and wrote a set of rules, *Regula Monachorum*, which have been read aloud every day and pondered in many Benedictine monasteries for over 1,400 years. Why is it that these monasteries and their Rule have survived when just about every other organization has folded or been absorbed or changed out of all recognition? The answer is partly because of the transparent spiritual depth of the Rule, the unchanging concept that the most important 'work' of the community is regular prayer. Another reason is the corresponding flexibility of the Rule regarding material matters which Benedict realized would change from age to age. It is marvellously practical and specific, but flexible. For example, it specifies that the monks shall drink half a pint of wine per day but notes that this should be modified 'if summer heat calls for more'.[36]

With regard to participative working, the subject of this chapter, the Rule states that the Abbot, equivalent to today's manager, shall be appointed by the Brothers over whom he is to have jurisdiction.[37] He is not appointed by an outside body of shareholders or money people. Regarding decision-making, chapter 3 states:

> As often as anything important is to be done in the monastery (*enterprise*?), the Abbot (*manager*?) shall call the whole community together and himself (*or herself*?) explain what the business is; and after hearing the advice of the brothers (*members, employee-owners*?) let him (*or her*?) ponder it and follow what he (*or she*?) judges to be the wisest course. The reason we have said all should be called for counsel is that the Lord often reveals what is better to the younger. The brothers (*members*?), for their part, are to express their opinions with all humility and not to defend their own ideas obstinately . . .[38]

Some of the major social reforms since the Rochdale Pioneers have been prefigured by monastic orders. For example, long before the Education Acts of 1887 and 1902 introduced universal education, there were monks and nuns dedicated to high standards of teaching for all within their orbit. Long before universal health care came into being as the National Health Service in 1948, there were orders dedicated to nursing people from all walks of life, especially the old and infirm.

A similar major reform is now needed to make the centennial change from capital-ownership to the mutuality of employee-ownership. It would be a legitimate role for a contemporary monastic order to commit itself to this task. It could be taken up by an existing order or it could be new. Let us call it the Order of Co-operative Companions (OCC). It would bring together men and women to form a pool from which co-operative businesses could draw. The members of the OCC would come to the co-operative as workers, not specifically as consultants or paid advisers. Some might have entrepreneurial skills to help to initiate a new business and then move on; others might stay a longer time and become members of the co-operative. The OCC would work in any capacity required, offering competence, flexibility and unswerving commitment to co-operative principles. It would draw its inspiration from communities like Iona, and churches such as the Mennonites for social justice, and from Taizé for servant-leadership. Although the OCC is envisaged as a specifically Christian order with a rule and lifestyle similar to the Benedictines or Franciscans, the members of the order would be available to work in any co-operative business, whether or not it has a religious foundation. The OCC is to serve the co-operative movement and it needs only one or two people to initiate it.

Conclusion

The industrial society which we have so assiduously developed is hardly more than 200 years old, a short time in the face of the millennium and the span of human history. The turning-points for work structures and ownership, such as the early Companies Acts and the Industrial and Provident Societies Acts for co-operatives, were passed less than 150 years ago.[39] On this timescale it is unsurprising that we are in a state of flux, as Marx foresaw, and it is correspondingly encouraging that there will be opportunities to make changes for the better during the coming century. Few are converted to Christianity by reading books. More often we are brought to conviction because we see the outcome of faith in other people's lives. We respond to the incarnational witness. So also with employee-ownership: few will take up such a contrasting commercial culture by listening to a lecture, but some who seek abundance and enrichment in their working lives may be moved to look further into the matter.

So, let us ensure that the rising generation of entrepreneurs are aware of this contrasting culture. Let us demonstrate with conviction in the 1,000 and more co-operatives now trading that employee-ownership is not only a contribution to a more just society but also practicable and sustainable in the economic culture in which we are placed. Let greyheads not cling on to power for too long, but affirm and nurture the idealism inherent in younger people. Let us tend the spark of employee-ownership fire and support the servant-leaders.

Notes

1 Some co-operative enterprises regard the chairperson's casting vote as undemocratic, and exclude it by rule.

2 Arthur Bryant, *English Saga* (London, 1940), 215.

3 Industrial and Provident Societies Act 1965, Section 1(3).

4 *Industrial Co-operatives: A Guide to the ICOM Model Rules* (ICOM, 1977), Rule 2, objects, 7.

[5] In Britain universal suffrage was finally accepted in 1928 when all women over 21 received the vote. In USA, the 19th Amendment to the US Constitution was passed in 1920.

[6] Genesis 25: 29–34.

[7] Adam Smith, *The Theory of Moral Sentiments*, quoted in Robert Heilbroner, *The Worldly Philosophers* (New York, 1953), 74.

[8] A. Bonner, *British Co-operation* (Manchester, 1961), 61.

[9] Equivalent public figures a century later might be the former bishop of Durham, David Jenkins, and C. S. Lewis, author of *The Screwtape Letters*, but by this time there were fewer opportunities for academics to change the social order.

[10] J. Bailey, *The British Co-operative Movement* (London, 1955), 118.

[11] Industrial Common Ownership Movement (ICOM), 74 Kirkgate, Leeds LS2 7DJ.

[12] See note 4 above.

[13] J. Wallace, *A New Thing: The Story of Daily Bread Co-operative, 1975–1985* (Daily Bread Co-operative, Bedford Road, Northampton, NN1 7AD, 1986), 11.

[14] Equity Shoes, Leicester, is an example of a long-established producer co-operative in which control is no longer in the hands of the current employee-members.

[15] De-regulation Order (Industrial and Provident Societies Act) 1996, amends Section 2(1)(a) of the 1965 Act.

[16] 'John Lewis is not up for sale, says Chairman', *Independent* (14 August 1999).

[17] *Co-operative Businesses in the UK, 1993 Directory* (Leeds ICOM and Open University, 1993), p. xi.

[18] D. Goodhart, 'Don't mind the gap', *Prospect* (August–September 1999), 12.

[19] Population of Africa, 750 million (*Collins Dictionary*); average cost of food, US$1.4 per week = US$73 per annum. Cost of food for whole continent = US$55 billion per annum.

[20] H. Elliott (ed.), *Letters of J. S. Mill* (London, 1910), letter to Park Godwin, January 1869.

[21] Matthew 5: 14.

[22] There is also a celebration of Holy Communion/Lord's Supper every fortnight.

[23] Acts 4: 34, 'There was no one in the group who was in need.'

[24] Heilbroner, *The Worldly Philosophers*, 142, commenting on Engels's *The Condition of the Working Class in England in 1844.*

[25] Marx, 1818–83; Engels, 1820–95.

[26] Karl Marx and Friedrich Engels, *The Communist Manifesto*, quoted in Heilbroner, *The Wordly Philosophers*, 148.

[27] *Yearbook of Co-operative Enterprise 1996* (Plunkett Foundation, 1996), 201.

[28] E. F. Schumacher, *Small is Beautiful* (London, 1973).

[29] Triodos Bank, 11 The Promenade, Bristol, BS8 3NN.

[30] The Ecology Building Society, 18 Station Road, Cross Hills, Keighley, West Yorkshire, BD20 7EH.

[31] *ICOF: The First Twenty-five Years* (ICOF, 227 City Road, London EC1V 1JT).

[32] Ethical Investment Research and Information Service (EIRIS), 80–4 Broadway, London, SW8 1SF.

[33] R. Greenleaf, *The Servant Leader* (Indianapolis, 1970), available from Greenleaf Center for Servant Leadership, 921 East 86th Street, Indianapolis, IN 46240, USA. Greenleaf's philosophical writings on servant-leadership have influenced two generations of entrepreneurs and managers.

[34] Isaiah 42: 1–4.

[35] Matthew 20: 25–8.

[36] *The Rule of St Benedict in English*, ed. Timothy Fry, OSB (Collegeville, MN, 1981), ch. 40.

[37] Ibid., ch. 64, re The Institution of the Abbot: 'he should be appointed whom the united community chooses in the fear of God'.

[38] Ibid., ch. 3.

[39] Companies Act 1855; Industrial and Provident Societies Act 1852.

5

Amish economics: the interface of religious values and economic interests

DONALD B. KRAYBILL

Overview

The Amish are one of the more colourful and distinctive religious subcultures in North America. They trace their roots to the Anabaptist movement of the sixteenth century that emerged in the context of the Protestant Reformation in south Germany and Switzerland.[1] The Amish were part of the Swiss Brethren wing of the Anabaptist movement, sometimes called the radical reformation, which originated in 1525. They formed their own distinctive identity under the leadership of Jacob Ammann. This Swiss Brethren leader and his followers called for renewal in congregational life, which in 1693 led to the formation of an Amish branch of the Anabaptist family.

The Amish migrated to North America in the eighteenth and nineteenth centuries in search of freedom from religious persecution, of political stability and of productive farmland.[2] During their sojourn in North America, their community life and social organization have been anchored on an agrarian base regulated by the seasonal cycles and vagaries of the weather. They have resisted industrialization and until recently virtually all of their members were employed in agriculture or in closely related trades. An overwhelming majority of their households operated small family-owned farms. This similar occupational base gave rise to a homogeneous, virtually single-class society.

In the last two decades of the twentieth century the Amish have rapidly begun developing microenterprises in many of their larger settlements.[3] Indeed in some settlements more than 50 per cent of the adults are involved in Amish-owned businesses of one sort or another. This rapid and dramatic move into the world of business and commerce is the most significant social change in Amish society since they first disembarked in North America in the early eighteenth century. Such an occupational transformation provides an interesting case-study because the Amish are not merely abandoning their ploughs for profitable jobs in mainstream industry, but are establishing their own microenterprises where they can control the terms and conditions of their work outside of an agrarian context.[4] They are creating their own industries within the constraints of their distinctive ethnic culture in ways that give the newly created businesses a unique Amish identity. This chapter traces the rise of the economic patterns associated with Amish microenterprises and argues that they are negotiated cultural outcomes that embody distinctive Amish values.

Distinctive cultural practices

Amish social organization is shaped by some distinctive cultural values and practices. The Amish own private property but they also espouse communal commitments for the common good of their ethnic community. Farmers and business owners hold property and buy and sell products in the larger market-place much like other Americans, but many distinctive Amish values regulate their economic practices and views.

As heirs of the Anabaptist movement, the Amish have long emphasized separation from the larger social world – the world of politics, consumerism, entertainment and leisure. As a communal group they restrain individualism and place the priorities of the community and the common good over the rights of the individual. Hence individuals are taught to eschew pride and above all to practise the virtues of humility, obedience, self-denial and modesty in a spirit of deference to the expectations of their community. This deliberate rejection of the ideology of individualism sets the Amish apart from the core value of American culture and makes them a distinctive counter-culture in the larger North American society. Their commitment to the priority of community and their separation from the larger culture leads to a variety of unique Amish practices.[5]

Distinctive Amish costume articulates the group's separation from the larger world on a daily basis. Wearing ethnic garb not only draws lines of social separation; it also enhances solidarity within the ethnic enclave. In addition to the garb itself, married men grow beards but not moustaches, and adult women wear a prayer covering or bandanna throughout the day. Members speak a Pennsylvania German dialect within the circle of family and community but speak English when interacting with outsiders. Education is typically limited to eight years in a one-room primary school operated by Amish families.[6] Worship services are held in homes, not in church buildings. The basic unit of social organization beyond the extended family is the church district – a bounded geographical area in which some twenty-five to thirty-five families reside, work, fellowship and worship together.

The Amish use modern technology selectively. Their rejection of some forms of technology is based on their principle of separation from the world as well as on their unwavering commitment to the solidarity of their community. They fear that some forms of technology will fragment their community and unduly expose members to outside influences and vices. For example, they forbid members to own and operate motor vehicles, but they do permit them to hire vehicles (with a driver) for long-distance travel and business purposes. Horse-and-buggy transportation reinforces face-to-face interaction, keeps members tethered to their local geographical community, and symbolizes a sharp separation from the larger society. The automobile – self-(Gk *autos*) mobility – in Amish eyes is a tool of individualism that offers unrestricted mobility which in time would pull their community asunder. In most settlements horses rather than tractors are used for power in the fields because Amish elders fear that tractor farming will lead to technologically advanced farms which will take work from Amish youth and eventually lead to the demise of the family farm.

Other key restrictions include taboos on communicative technology such as televisions, radios, computers and videos, all of which would expose members directly to the values of the larger society and in time might contaminate Amish convictions. Early in the twentieth century the Amish church forbade the use of 110-volt electricity from public utility lines but did allow the use of 12-volt electricity from batteries. This distinction continues today.

Face-to-face interaction is the foundation of social solidarity in

Amish life. Thus telephones were deemed unnecessary in the early decades of the century but by mid-century community phones, shared by several families, were permitted at the end of farm lanes. Today telephones are permitted for business and farming uses in some settlements but are typically not installed in homes. The use of mobile cellular phones has blurred the traditional boundaries and created considerable controversy in some settlements.[7] The bulk of the technological restrictions in Amish life are designed to build community solidarity. Although Amish do employ considerable state-of-the-art technology, they reject those forms which they fear would lead to an erosion and fragmentation of the soul of their community. The commitments arising from their guidelines are clear: technology should serve the community, not vice versa.

Amish settlements today are located in twenty-three states, primarily in the mid-central and eastern region of the United States and in the Canadian province of Ontario. More than 1,200 church districts (congregations) are located in some 250 geographical settlements.[8] Today in North America, the Amish number about 180,000 people including adults and children. Youth under twenty-one years of age compose about half of the community.[9] The Amish practise adult baptism and typically baptize new members between the ages of eighteen and twenty-two. The Amish population is growing, indeed doubling, about every twenty to twenty-five years. The growth is fuelled not by converts from the outside but by large families of seven to eight children on the average and by retention rates that hover around 85 per cent. Large families and strong retention rates combine to make the Amish a growing, thriving and dynamic religious subculture in North America.

The rise of microenterprises

Over the generations, the Amish have been a people of the land. Their community organization, family structure, social values and church life were rooted in agriculture. Until recently they were rural peasants who perpetuated their distinctive lifestyle in rural enclaves in the shadows of the industrial revolution. In many ways their world-view and economic organization typified pre-industrial patterns.

In the last two decades of the twentieth century, in some of their older and larger settlements, barefoot Amish farmers have become enterprising entrepreneurs without the benefit of high school, let alone college, or other formal training in marketing, accounting or management. Without a business plan, hundreds of former farmers have become successful entrepreneurs. Indeed in the large Lancaster (Pennsylvania) settlement as many as 1,500 Amish own and operate their own businesses. The development of microenterprises is most heavily concentrated in the older settlements such as Lancaster County, PA, and Holmes County, OH.[10]

What prompted this rather sudden rise of Amish businesses? In the late 1970s and early 1980s some of the Amish settlements located near urban areas faced a demographic crisis of sorts. They were being squeezed by the rapid growth of their own communities on the one side and by the rising cost of farmland on the other. Farmland prices were driven up because land was becoming increasingly scarce due to industrialization, urban sprawl and tourism. A variety of options offered the Amish relief from the demographic crisis: (1) migration to other areas; (2) subdivision of farms; (3) purchase of new farmland; (4) non-Amish employment; (5) higher education; or (6) artificial birth control. A few families left some of the older settlements to establish new ones in other counties and states, but many families were reluctant to leave the homesteads of their youth and the land that their ancestors had settled and farmed for generations. Some migration did occur but it was not enough to alleviate the demographic quandary. In Lancaster County, PA, many farms were subdivided to accommodate two families on the same amount of land with more intensive farming practices, but farms cannot be divided forever and still remain viable. Additional farmland was purchased on the edge of some settlements but the high cost of land made it financially difficult to operate a farm.

Another ready option was employment in large industrial factories in nearby urban areas. The Amish, however, were reluctant to have their youth and fathers working away from home in an alien cultural environment. Moreover, they worried that some of the employee benefit programmes might erode the dependence of members on the church and interfere with the mutual aid activities of the community. The primary fear was that factory work would intrude and contaminate Amish values and erode their social separation from the larger society.

Use of artificial birth control to limit family size was not a viable option because the Amish considered birth control an act of tampering with divine providence – usurping the will of God. Permitting youth to enter higher education and prepare for professional vocations would have opened new avenues for employment, but church leaders feared that higher education would cultivate an individualism and arrogance that would challenge the order and traditional authority of the community and eventually lead to its demise.

The development of microenterprises, however, was an option that the Amish decided to pursue. A formal decision by church leaders to embrace microenterprises was never made, but implicit approval was given to members who began developing small businesses. The rise of microenterprises was in many ways a negotiated cultural compromise. Yes, the Amish would abandon their cows and ploughs and leave their fields behind. But no, they would not enter the ranks of modern factory workers and sell their souls to corporate America. Instead, they would create their own industrial revolution by establishing miniature factories that they themselves would own and operate. In this context they could control the terms and conditions of their labour and ensure that their new form of economic organization would stay within the moral order of Amish culture. Thus, in many ways, the microenterprises are a result of Amish negotiations with modernity.

Despite the rise of business endeavours, many members in all of the major settlements continue to farm and maintain a vigorous agricultural economy today. The Amish, in other words, have not completely abandoned farming but have simply added small businesses alongside their farming operations. In some settlements the business operations have been so successful that they have generated a new source of capital which sometimes has been used to buy additional farmland even at expensive prices.

Microenterprise profile

The Amish ventures into business involve small manufacturing and woodworking shops, as well as residential and commercial construction crews that travel to worksites away from home. Some seasonal operations cater to tourists and sell items such as quilts, dolls, food and handicrafts. The bulk of the products, however, are manufactured and sold in public markets. Some products and certain businesses (for example, carriage manufacturing) serve primarily Amish customers, but most of the products are sold and distributed outside the Amish orbit. Although most of the enterprises operate independently of the agrarian economy, some are tied to farming. Machine repair shops and those that manufacture farm equipment, for example, are linked directly to the farm economy.[11]

Many of the businesses are located adjacent to a farming homestead. It is not uncommon for a father to retire from farming at forty-five years of age and start a business that provides work for several of his young and adult children. Another adult child may continue to operate the family farm adjacent to the business. Virtually all of the first generation of entrepreneurs were raised on a farm and simply moved into business without apprenticeship, technical training or formal education. Their experience in farming provided important values – independence, hard work, flexibility and risk-taking – which were easily transferred and applied to the world of business. These traits have served the new entrepreneurs well. The second generation of Amish entrepreneurs is now assuming ownership of many of the businesses at the turn of the twenty-first century. Many of them have developed their entrepreneurial and managerial skills through apprenticeships in businesses operated by their parents or other extended family members.

Amish women own and operate about 20 per cent of the Amish enterprises in the Lancaster County, PA, settlement. This pattern, which is probably the case in other Amish settlements as well, will surely lead to a change in gender roles in what has traditionally been a patriarchal society. Amish women tend to operate businesses that specialize in household-related products – quilts, handicrafts, dried flowers and food products. Many, but not all, of these businesses cater to tourists, who represent a ready and hungry market near some of the larger settlements.

The success and sales of the microenterprises are robust. Annual sales for many of the businesses exceed $100,000 and it is likely that at least 10 per cent have sales topping a million dollars.

Customer and product patterns vary from business to business. Some shops cater primarily to tourists, others to the Amish, and still others to markets beyond the immediate region. Many manufacturers have mixed markets and sell products to both the retail and wholesale trade. In recent years Amish entrepreneurs have increasingly turned to various forms of advertising to promote their products. In some communities non-Amish marketers publish an annual directory of Amish businesses and mail it to wholesale buyers across the country. In Lancaster, PA, each spring a two-day trade market provides an opportunity for hundreds of Amish entrepreneurs to display their products to wholesale buyers who come hundreds of miles in search of Amish products. A monthly newspaper, *Plain Communities Business Exchange*, serves the interests of Amish business owners in numerous states. Some non-Amish marketers are now selling Amish products through e-commerce on the World Wide Web.

Ready markets, distinctive products, good value and the hard work of Amish entrepreneurs have assured the remarkable success of Amish enterprises. The failure rate of Amish businesses is less than 5 per cent over a typical five-year period. This compares to a failure rate of nearly 60 per cent for American firms in the first six years of operation. Such success is even more remarkable given the technological restrictions, limited formal education and the recent entry of the Amish into the world of business.

Cultural resources

Cultural resources within the Amish community have been a prime source of their entrepreneurial success. The Amish have a heritage of entrepreneurial values rooted in their agrarian history. The wisdom gained from coping with the contingencies of the weather and the need to respond to daily problems on the farm have served new entrepreneurs well. Moreover, the strenuous work ethic cultivated over decades of tilling the soil has also benefited the needs of start-up industries. Amish austerity and a frugal lifestyle help to keep overhead costs low in business operations and subsequently translate into greater profits.

The vast majority of employees in Amish businesses are also Amish. A large ethnic labour pool of employees with similar values provides a homogeneous ethos that enhances productivity.

Many children begin working in various roles in the business while they are still in elementary school. When they terminate formal schooling at fourteen years of age, many begin to work full-time in a family enterprise. This amounts to a system of apprenticeship so that by the time they are seventeen or eighteen Amish young people have not only mastered one or more trade skills but they are also familiar with the operation and management of a business. Indeed, some of them begin operating their own business in their late teens or early twenties. The vast and growing pool of ethnic labour and the informal system of apprenticeship provide valuable cultural resources for the growth of Amish business.

Cultural restraints

The moral order of Amish culture also places many restraints on economic life. Some of the restrictions, ironically, are likely to have bolstered the growth and success of Amish businesses. Amish entrepreneurs are constrained somewhat by, among other things, family life, sacred days, technological limitations, the size of enterprises, types of products and acceptable occupations. The family is the primary social unit in Amish society and strong cultural values operate to keep businesses close to and subservient to family concerns. The church strongly frowns on mothers with small children working away from home. The church also prefers fathers to work at home as much as possible so that they can be role models for their children and collaborate with their spouses in raising and disciplining the children. Whenever possible, business people try to involve their family in the operation of the business with the hopes that the business will unite, not divide the family.

The church strictly prohibits any commercial activity on Sunday. Amish businesses can often be identified on back country roads by signs that announce 'No Sunday Sales'. Some owners also distribute business cards that say 'No Sunday Sales'. Beyond Sabbath restrictions the Amish also observe other sacred days that are typically not honoured by American retail stores. These days include a second day for Christmas and Easter observance, Ascension day, Pentecost Monday and a day of fasting in autumn. Festive wedding days also bring 'closed' signs to many Amish shops.

Beyond these temporal restrictions the moral order of Amish life limits the products and types of business that are acceptable. It would be off limits for an Amish business to sell televisions, repair computers or produce videos. Likewise, jobs that involve frequent travel away from home, flying in aircraft, participation in political organizations or working in the entertainment industry are outside permissible boundaries. Amish businesses by and large must operate within the acceptable moral order of Amish culture. Radio and television advertising is not possible for Amish entrepreneurs. Litigation is forbidden in Amish society because in their eyes it is a form of force which contradicts the teachings of Jesus to love the enemy and turn the other cheek. Thus, while Amish entrepreneurs will use attorneys to prepare legal agreements and to represent them in zoning hearings, they are not permitted to hire attorneys to conduct litigation on their behalf. All of these traditional ethical practices of the church place constraints on Amish entrepreneurial activity, but they are not the most severe constraints. Restrictions on the size of business operations and on various forms of technology bring the greatest handicaps.

One of the most salient features of Amish businesses is their commitment to small-scale operations. Only 6 per cent of Amish businesses have seven or more full-time employees. Although there are not explicit and specific limitations to the size of operations, the church clearly opposes 'big business'. The Amish fear large operations for several reasons. First, they worry that large operations will weaken the involvement of the immediate family. In the pursuit of growth, entrepreneurs may be tempted to focus all their energy on the business, which will soon outgrow the needs and interests of their extended family. Second, the church worries that larger businesses will pull them into the larger commercial world and create more temptations to use technology, become entangled with government and use litigation. Third, Amish leaders fear that sizeable operations will cultivate conceit as entrepreneurs take pride in their successful achievements. Such pride would erode the fundamental values of Amish culture – humility, modesty and obedience. Finally, large businesses are more likely to concentrate considerable wealth in the hands of the owner and thus disrupt the delicate balance of social equality in the community. Consequently, the church frowns on large businesses and will sanction entrepreneurs whose businesses become too big, even though the exact limits of size are somewhat ambiguous. It is most important that wealthy entrepreneurs do not show off or flaunt their wealth in self-serving or self-aggrandizing ways.

Interestingly, the limitation on size has spread Amish entrepreneurship far and wide across the Amish community. Instead of concentrating hundreds of Amish employees in several large Amish factories, hundreds of small shops provide a meaningful work environment for employees without the virus of alienation so common in the modern workplace. The limitation on size decentralizes operations and encourages the rise of many manufacturing sites that give hundreds of owners the challenge and satisfaction of entrepreneurship.

Technological compromises

At first blush restrictions on technology appear to be the most limiting handicap to the success of Amish business. How can a business be competitive and profitable if motor vehicles, electricity, computers and telephones are taboo? One of the more remarkable features of Amish economic organization is the way in which the traditional moral code has been adapted to meet the needs of commercial operations.[12] The resulting technological adaptations, which at first glance look downright silly to outsiders, represent creative cultural compromises that respect traditional Amish norms while at the same time providing enough space to benefit from the fruits of science. Negotiating with modernity, so to speak, the Amish have created technological compromises that enable their businesses to thrive within the traditional moral boundaries of their community.

The taboo on owning and operating motor vehicles has been long standing in Amish life. As the settlements began to grow in mid-century, church leaders permitted members to hire a non-Amish neighbour to drive them to funerals, weddings or other social gatherings at a distance. As businesses grew in recent years, the practice of hiring motor vehicles became even more pronounced. Thus, many business owners hire trucks and vans on a daily basis to haul products and conduct business. In concert with some other technological practices, the Amish often make a distinction between use and ownership. Members may be permitted to use some forms of technology but not to own them. In this way the church is able to exercise some control over the technology.

Electricity is, of course, an important source of energy for most businesses. The church had placed a taboo on 110-volt electricity from public utility lines since the second decade of the twentieth century. The advent of television and other modern household conveniences confirmed the wisdom of this taboo in the mind of elders as the twentieth century unfolded. But how could a business be powered without electricity? Amish mechanics discovered that they could remove the electric motors from manufacturing equipment and replace them with hydraulic or pneumatic motors. This solution, nicknamed 'Amish electric', was acceptable to the church in some settlements because it provided power for the shops without violating the proscription on electrical usage. Thus, today in many Amish communities a diesel engine sits in a shed adjoining the shop and provides power to operate hydraulic and/or air pumps. These pumps circulate oil or air under pressure, as the case may be, via hoses attached to the hydraulic or pneumatic motors that power heavy manufacturing equipment. In this fashion and with the aid of 'Amish electricity', the Amish are able to operate modern shop equipment which makes them productive and enables them to remain rather competitive.

In the late 1980s church leaders in some settlements forbade the ownership of personal computers for fear they would lead to television. Church leaders also prohibited members from using the internet as it developed. The principle of use versus ownership undergirds the arrangement that some Amish business owners have with outside providers who sell computer-generated payroll and inventory services to them. In this manner Amish business owners can have access to computerized information services for management purposes although their manufacturing equipment is not computerized.

The rise of Amish businesses also encouraged a broader use of the telephone. The actual location of telephones and the norms governing their use vary considerably from settlement to settlement. In some conservative settlements telephones are not permitted, but in many of them they may be used for business purposes. In some cases they are installed inside the businesses but in many cases they are placed in a small shed, or adjacent to a business. A fairly firm taboo restricts them from being installed in homes in virtually all of the settlements.

Many of these technological compromises appear baffling if not downright contradictory to outsiders. But within the context of Amish society these unique arrangements have been creative solutions that have permitted Amish businesses to grow and thrive within the boundaries of the moral order of their culture.

Lessons from the Amish

The story of Amish enterprise shows the delicate interplay between religious values and economic interests. The Amish experience demonstrates the powerful role and influence of religious values in shaping economic organization. The size, texture and ethos of Amish business are very unique and distinctive because they have been shaped, constrained and guided by religious values and commitments. Patterns of Amish social organization will surely change with the emergence of microenterprises, but religious interests have clearly constrained the direction of economic development, and in this way the Amish provide clear empirical evidence that challenges the assumptions of economic determinism.

The Amish are also instructive for the priority they place on the welfare and solidarity of their community. Rather than yielding to individualism or economic determinism, they ask if a particular technology or economic practice will build community or erode it, contribute to community solidarity or undercut it. New technologies which fortify community are welcomed but those that are a menace to the common good are banned. Contemporary society, with its penchant for materialist patterns of consumer consumption, values the newest, the biggest and the most powerful technological gadgets and gives little attention to their possible social impact or their possible toll on the bonds of community. The Amish remind us that, in the final analysis, technology and economic practice ought to be designed and deployed to serve the long-term interests of the common good of human communities.

The Amish also teach us to value the collective wisdom that accumulates in the cultural reservoir of a community over the centuries. They teach us to appreciate the limits of individualistic perspective and the shallow fulfilment found in immediate technological gratification. The Amish reliance on collective wisdom underscores the fickle and unreliable nature of much individualistic human knowledge. Their experience also attests to the importance and role of a religious tradition in building enduring human communities. And by their example, the Amish would argue that membership in an enduring community is the essential and necessary commitment that promises meaning, identity and belonging, scarce commodities as they may be, in the midst of a post-modern context.

Notes

1 Introductions to Amish history are provided by John A. Hostetler, *Amish Society* (Baltimore, 1993), and Steven M. Nolt, *A History of the Amish* (Intercourse, PA, 1992).

2 The last Amish congregation in Europe became extinct in 1936.

3 The story of this development is told by Donald B. Kraybill and Steven M. Nolt, *Amish Enterprise: From Plows to Profits* (Baltimore, 1995).

4 An exception to this trend is the Amish settlement in northern Indiana where many members work in large factories that manufacture recreational vehicles. These factories are owned by non-Amish but are located near Amish communities in rural areas in order to attract Amish labour. Thomas J. Meyers, 'Lunch pails and factories', in Donald B. Kraybill and Marc A. Olshan (eds.), *The Amish Struggle with Modernity* (Hanover, NH, 1994), 165–81, charts the development of the Amish involvement in these industries.

5 Distinctive Amish practices are described by Hostetler, *Amish Society*, and Donald B. Kraybill, *The Riddle of Amish Culture*, rev. edn (Baltimore, 2001), and idem, *The Puzzles of Amish Life* (Intercourse, PA, 1998).

6 Gertrude E. Huntington, 'Persistence and change in Amish education', in Kraybill and Olshan, *The Amish Struggle with Modernity*, 77–96, provides a helpful overview of persistent themes as well as changing ones in the schooling practices of the Amish in North America.

7 The story of the Amish struggle with the telephone is told from a communications perspective by Diane Zimmerman Umble, *Holding the Line: The Telephone in Old Order Mennonite and Amish Life* (Baltimore, 1996).

[8] A complete listing of all the Amish settlements in North America can be found in David Luthy, 'Amish migration patterns: 1972–1992', in Kraybill and Olshan, *The Amish Struggle with Modernity*, 243–60.

[9] My estimates of the Amish population are principally derived from a directory of Amish ministers published by Ben Raber (ed.), *The New American Almanac* (Baltic, OH, 2000). This directory of Amish church districts and ordained leaders is updated and published annually.

[10] Many of the observations and the numerical data in this essay come from a major study of microenterprises conducted in the Lancaster County, PA, settlement by Kraybill and Nolt, *Amish Enterprise*. The investigators interviewed 114 owners of all the Amish businesses in thirteen different church districts. Although rooted in personal observations of the Lancaster community, the descriptions and analysis that I provide in this chapter are applicable to many of the larger Amish settlements in North America. For comparative studies of business developments in different Amish communities, see various chapters in the *Amish Struggle with Modernity* by Kraybill and Olshan. For comparisons of Amish industries in the two different settlements in Pennsylvania see the work of Donald B. Kraybill and Conrad L. Kanagy, 'From milk to manufacturing: the rise of entrepreneurship in two old order Amish communities', *Mennonite Quarterly Review*, 70 (1996), 263–80.

[11] In the Lancaster, PA, settlement there are actually two directories of Amish businesses that are updated and distributed annually: *The Lancaster County Business Directory* and the *Dutch Business Directory*. Both publications are slick state-of-the-art publications with colour photographs of Amish products. They include advertisements for several hundred Amish businesses. These directories provide an excellent overview of the variety and sophistication of Amish products. In the Holmes County area of Ohio, the *Ohio Amish Business Directory* lists Amish businesses and sells advertising space to Amish entrepreneurs.

[12] In *The Riddle of Amish Culture* I devote several chapters to explaining the unique cultural compromises that the Amish have made as they adapted their traditional practices to modern life.

6

The pursuit of values in international trade

ISABELLA D. BUNN

My inspiration for reflecting on the pursuit of values in international trade probably lies in the price of Polish electrified golf cars sold in America, if we pretended they were manufactured and sold in Canada. This case was, for me, an early lesson on the types of values that are protected within the international economic system. It also indicated some of the strains in justifying such protection.

In a 1974 action before the United States International Trade Commission, American producers of golf cars complained that electric golf cars from Poland were being sold at less than fair value within the meaning of the Anti-dumping Act.[1] This is one of the key laws intended to combat so-called 'unfair trade': if imports are being sold at less than fair value, and such sales injure US industry, an anti-dumping duty may be imposed to offset this price advantage. Because Poland was a non-market economy, the determination of what a fair price might be was based on the sales price of similar merchandise for home consumption in a free country. In this case, Canada was chosen and, after an elaborate set of calculations, a determination of dumping was made against Poland.

At the time, I felt a mild sense of confusion and frustration. How can it be that the law goes through all these contortions to limit the imports of a few hundred golf cars, when so many more obvious instances of economic injustice go unremedied? Maybe it is unfair that certain golf cars are sold too cheaply, but surely it is more unfair that hundreds of millions of people go to bed hungry every night. Today, I understand the rationale behind anti-dumping actions better than I did twenty-five years ago. But some frustration about the limitations of international trade law has stayed with me and encouraged me to investigate the subject.

The topic of the linkage between international trade and values is a large and growing one. At the popular level, the scholarly level and policy-making level, there is a new language of 'trade and . . .': trade and the environment; trade and human rights; trade and child labour; trade and culture; trade and competition; trade and public health; trade and animal welfare; trade and poverty. There is also a large and growing constituency giving voice to 'trade and . . .' concerns. The debate is evolving among many players: grass-roots consumer groups, trade unions, companies concerned with social responsibility, academics and scientists of various disciplines, a range of non-governmental organizations and activists, departments of national governments, and regional and international governmental organizations. To be sure, the debate expands beyond trading relations to broader economic and ethical questions of government regulation, investment, financial flows, aid, debt; indeed, to overall critiques of the market system and the process of globalization.

The media has captured some of this debate, building on our awareness. The following types of headlines, which were largely unknown a decade ago, are now familiar:[2]

> Sweatshops rampant in the garment industry . . .
> Oil company seeks to dump toxic chemicals at sea . . .
> Bonded servitude exposed in India . . .
> Child pornography disseminated on the Internet . . .
> Diamond trade linked to African warlords . . .
> Sex tourism promoted in Thailand . . .
> Bootleg CDs pull China into trade war . . .
> Turkish guest-workers sell own kidneys for cash . . .
> Chemical weapons technology smuggled into Iraq . . .
> Environmental activists destroy suspected GM crop . . .
> Poultry production techniques denounced as cruel . . .
> We Don't Want War . . . [The *Sun*'s message to the French on the beef ban]

In short, some of today's most troublesome headlines put two themes in the spotlight: values and international trade. They provoke us to think about potential restrictions on certain types of trade, and about measures to alleviate some of the negative social consequences of trade. From a Christian perspective, we are challenged by the need to respect human dignity, to exercise responsible stewardship over creation and to uphold justice and fairness, especially for the poor and oppressed.[3]

Within this vast topic, I would like to focus on the relatively narrow area of trade law. Such law involves a complex interaction between national, bilateral, regional and international levels of regulation. My main attention will be on the World Trade Organization (WTO), which in a sense regulates those who regulate international trade. While the WTO is designed to preserve a range of economic values (for example, it authorizes anti-dumping actions such as those used against Polish golf cars), my particular concern will be with non-economic values.

By way of introduction, I will discuss the predecessor to the WTO, the General Agreement on Tariffs and Trade (GATT), and some of the cornerstone values associated with it. I will then review the most recent round of trade negotiations under the GATT, the Uruguay Round, which resulted in the formation of the WTO. Again, I will look to the values embraced in this important new context. I will then examine, ever so briefly, five areas of values to assess their treatment under the world trading regime. These include public morals, assistance to developing countries, the environment, labour standards and human rights. Of course, the scope of this discussion precludes consideration of many important categories of moral issues related to trade, ranging from preserving national culture to protecting public health, to maintaining controls on exports of arms and nuclear material. Next, I will suggest the limitations of using the WTO and international trade law in the pursuit of certain values. I will also indicate some important cautions against resorting to trade restrictions as leverage for policy changes in a target country.

Finally, I will comment on the prospects for a new round of trade negotiations under the WTO. Major anti-globalization protests derailed plans for the so-called Millennium Round, which was to be launched in December 1999. The issue continues to be in the international media spotlight, and the controversy is raising further questions about the appropriate linkages between trade and values.

The General Agreement on Tariffs and Trade

The origins of the GATT lie with the establishment of a post-war international economic order. At the 1944 Bretton Woods conference, the International Monetary Fund and the International Bank for Reconstruction and Development (now called the World Bank) were founded. It was anticipated that a third agency, the International Trade Organization (ITO) would form the final plank of this new platform. Due to political objections, the ITO never materialized. However, the interim agreement that countries had negotiated, the General Agreement on Tariffs and Trade (GATT), emerged *de facto* as the world's trade forum.[4]

A major rationale for the establishment of the GATT was to avoid the protectionism, retaliation and trade wars of the 1930s. Its basic underlying philosophy is that open markets, non-discrimination and global competition in international trade are conducive to the national welfare of all countries. Of course, this also holds an important political dimension. The economic dislocations of the 1930s were seen as contributory factors to the Second World War. Increased prosperity was expected to reduce the scope for political tensions and a forum for negotiating trade conflicts was intended to keep them from spilling over into other areas. Thus, in addition to supporting economic objectives, the GATT helped underpin the goal of international peace and stability.

The GATT, headquartered in Geneva, deals with the actions of governments, and establishes disciplines in trade policy matters such as tariffs, quotas, subsidies and state trading. It is not expressly concerned with the behaviour of private businesses. Also, while the GATT embraces elements of a free-trade and market-driven philosophy, nowhere is 'free trade' cited as an ultimate goal of the trading system. Indeed, much of the GATT pertains to safeguards for domestic interests and regulatory regimes. To a large extent, tensions between domestic policies which may restrict trade and the GATT goals to liberalize trade underlie the debate on the pursuit of values in the international trading system.

Over the course of four decades, eight rounds of multilateral trade negotiations have been held under the auspices of the GATT. The first five were largely concerned with reduction of tariffs and quotas. The Kennedy Round, which began in 1964, and the Tokyo Round, which began in 1973, moved into the more difficult areas of non-tariff barriers. The most far-reaching set of multilateral trade negotiations was the Uruguay Round, to which I now turn.

The Uruguay Round and the establishment of the World Trade Organization

The Uruguay Round of trade negotiations was launched in Punta del Este in 1986 and concluded in 1994.[5] In addition to the further reduction of barriers in the form of tariffs and quotas, it continued the process of addressing a range of non-tariff barriers. One difficulty is that such barriers are by their nature less transparent and less quantifiable. Also, as they often take the form of government regulation, they are intricately entwined with a country's values and its exercise of sovereignty. Add to this the fact that the Uruguay Round considered a wide range of new and complex subjects, and the agreement itself represents quite a remarkable achievement. The WTO reports that this was not only the largest trade negotiation ever, but most probably the largest negotiation of any kind in history.

Three results of the Uruguay Round, out of more than 26,000 pages of final agreements, might be highlighted in particular. First, effective from 1 January 1995, the WTO was established. The GATT became one of the constituent agreements under the WTO. In addition to improved organizational visibility and efficiency, the new WTO structure provides an effective dispute-settlement mechanism.

Secondly, a new range of subjects came within the discipline of the WTO for the first time. Paralleling the GATT which covers trade in goods, a General Agreement on Trade in Services (GATS) and an Agreement on Trade-Related Intellectual Property Rights (TRIPs) were negotiated. Trade in agriculture and textiles and clothing were slated for reform. Attention was also devoted to natural resources, tropical products, investment measures and many other areas. This broadens the scope of trade covered by the WTO.

Thirdly, participation in the organization became increasingly important. During the course of the trade negotiations, some twenty-five new members joined. Today, there are 135 WTO members. China, one of the largest trading powers in the world, is currently being considered for membership. Again, this broadens the scope of trade covered by the WTO.

Before turning to a consideration of values under the WTO, it may be instructive to review what the WTO itself considers to be the value of the system in general.[6] As their website proclaims, 'There are many over-riding reasons why we're better off with the system than we would be without it.' The list of ten benefits includes:

(1) The system helps promote peace.
(2) Disputes are handled constructively.
(3) Rules make life easier for all.
(4) Freer trade cuts the cost of living.
(5) It provides more choice of products and qualities.
(6) Trade raises incomes.
(7) Trade stimulates economic growth.
(8) The basic principles make life more efficient.
(9) Governments are shielded from lobbying.
(10) The system encourages good government.

A critique of whether the stated benefits actually flow from the WTO system cannot be undertaken here. More fundamentally, as the debate on trade and values expands, the system will be under pressure from two directions: first, whether these 'benefits' (such as stimulation of economic growth) are always desirable, and second, what other types of benefits should be included in this list.

Values under the WTO system

The basic question is whether international trade law should be used to promote moral and social goals.[7] One of the overarching issues is that efforts either to liberalize or to restrict trade will inevitably result in winners and losers. For example, a lower tariff may mean an exporting country has a new market for its goods, leading to higher profits, increased foreign exchange and opportunities for development. Due to this competition, consumers in the importing country benefit from wider choices and greater affordability of products. But import-competing industries in that country may suffer from a diminished customer base, price and wage pressures, job losses and possibly even closure. If measures are taken to protect the domestic industry from foreign imports, consumers may face higher prices and overall industrial competitiveness may decline.

While the larger concerns of political economy cannot be addressed here, it should be borne in mind that the pursuit of values in international trade will cause disruption in existing economic relations. Moreover, many well-intended measures may be decried as disguised protectionism. I turn now to a brief consideration of five areas of values and their treatment under the WTO regime.

1. Protection of public morals

GATT Article XX(a) provides an exception to GATT rules for the 'protection of public morals'.[8] This rather vague language gives rise to two questions. First, what type of behaviour implicates public morals? Second, whose morals are to be protected – those of people in the importing country or those in the exporting country? The discussions surrounding the adoption of the GATT shed little light on these questions. But it is clear that for many years, both under bilateral treaties and national laws, governments have banned imports or exports for moral or humanitarian reasons. At the international level, two early examples of morally motivated trade restrictions include the General Act for the Suppression of the African Slave Trade (1890) and the International Opium Convention (1912).

The history of various national laws restricting trade on moral grounds makes for interesting reading: there have been bans on obscene prints, films of prize fights, violent pictures, lottery tickets, abortion-inducing drugs and items of a blasphemous character. Examples of current laws include the Israeli ban on the importation of non-kosher meat products, the US ban on interstate commerce in human organs, and the European Commission ban on the importation of skins of certain seal pups because of the public outrage over the method of killing. Examples of international efforts include limits on trade in certain endangered animal species and the ban on the manufacture, sale and use of land mines. Although the moral exception in trade policy reaches into broad areas of values, the overall scope of its application is rather limited.

2. Assistance to developing countries

The GATT initially had one main development-related provision: an infant-industry protection clause under Article XVIII. But as former colonies gained their political independence during the 1950s and 1960s, there came a growing awareness of economic inequality. In 1964, the United Nations Conference on Trade and Development was established to press for trade measures which would benefit developing countries. In 1965, a new section was added to the GATT entitled 'On Trade and Development'. One of the most significant outcomes of this was the adoption of a Generalized System of Preferences (GSP).[9] Under the GSP, industrialized countries were to grant tariff preferences to developing countries on a non-reciprocal basis. Such preferences are voluntary and unilateral, and their overall benefit over time has been debated. During the 1970s, more than seventy developing countries participated in the Tokyo Round of trade negotiations, and the concept of 'special and differential treatment' was adopted. Nonetheless, most developing countries abstained from signing the various Tokyo Round codes.

In the 1980s, the developing country stance towards the GATT shifted.[10] Reasons for this change include the debt crisis, advice from the World Bank and IMF, encouragement from the OECD, the example of rapid development in South East Asia, and the results of academic research. With a greater interest in gaining access to industrialized country markets came a willingness to engage in reciprocal bargaining. Thus, developing countries were active in the Uruguay Round and became more fully integrated into the multilateral system. All former members of the GATT signed on to the WTO and adopted the results of the negotiations. Indeed, part of the preamble to the Agreement Establishing the World Trade Organization recognizes 'that there is a need for positive efforts designed to ensure that developing countries, and especially the least developed among them, secure a share in the growth of international trade commensurate with the needs of their economic development'.

The principle of 'S & D', of Special and Differential Treatment for developing countries, continues to apply under the WTO in several important ways:[11]

(1) a lower level of obligations;
(2) more flexible implementation timetables;
(3) a lower threshold of 'best endeavour' commitments;
(4) more favourable treatment for least developed countries;
(5) availability of technical assistance and training.

Proponents of trade liberalization still caution that allowing developing countries to avoid reciprocal obligations deprives them of many of the benefits of WTO membership. To some commentators, the S & D strategy remains ill-advised, costly and often counter-productive.

Those concerned with the economic plight of the developing world might acknowledge some of these arguments, yet feel a growing frustration at the ineffectiveness of trade policy in dealing with international disparities. The recent *Human Development Report* published by the United Nations Development Program indicates that well over a billion people are deprived of basic consumption needs: 'Inequalities are stark. Globally, the 20% of the world's people in the highest income countries account for 86% of total private consumption expenditures – the poorest 20% a miniscule 1.3%.'[12] In seventy countries with nearly a billion people, consumption today is lower than it was twenty-five years ago. The spectacular growth of incomes for many people in Asia must be acknowledged, as must the role of liberalized international trade in spurring such growth. Yet only twenty-one developing countries worldwide achieved growth in GDP per capita of 3 per cent or more each year between 1995 and 1997. This is the crucial rate needed to set a frame for poverty reduction. There is a list of over sixty low-income countries in the back of this report, low income being defined as per capita GNP of $765 or less, in 1995.

So what should the international trading system do about this enormous problem? I would suggest that one useful exercise might be for the WTO to examine its conscience in what it has done and in what it has failed to do. In other words, to conduct a review of its policies in light of their impact on developing countries. For example, for many years the entire subject of agricultural trade was treated as 'special' and therefore off limits in trade negotiations. Efforts are now under way to bring this vast sector, which is riddled with anti-competitive policies and subsidies, within the WTO disciplines. A second area of great importance to developing countries is trade in textiles and clothing, which again has been subject to high levels of protectionism.

A further problem lies in some of the contradictory effects of WTO policy. As mentioned, one of the results of the Uruguay Round was the new discipline on intellectual property rights. Understandably, many developing countries were opposed to this on the simple basis that they were not major stakeholders of such property; they feared increased costs and reduced access to technology transfers. As Harvard economist Jeffrey Sachs cautions: 'The system of intellectual property rights must balance the need to provide incentives for innovation against the need of poor countries to get the results of innovation.'[13] Typical of this problem is the pressure on poor countries to provide patent protection for pharmaceutical products. This has undermined their ability to dispense low-cost medicines. In South Africa, for example, the costs of using patented AIDS treatment is so high that the government is likely to allow its own firms to manufacture the drugs, regardless of international patent violations.

Thus, as can be seen, the impact of trade negotiations on the developing world needs careful assessment from a variety of public policy perspectives. There is a Committee on Trade and Development within the WTO. There is also a new joint venture between the WTO and the World Bank to focus on trade and development issues.[14] They would do well to increase their scrutiny of some of these complex interrelationships. Indeed, perhaps the WTO should be challenged to add the provision of 'Greater economic and social justice, especially for the poorest countries' to its list of expected benefits of the trading system.

3. Preservation of the environment

There are two main provisions within the GATT agreement which focus upon environmental concerns. Like the provision on public morals, they are both found under Article XX as exceptions to the GATT. One allows measures 'necessary to protect human, animal or plant life or health'. The other allows measures 'relating to the conservation of exhaustible natural resources . . . made effective in conjunction with restrictions on domestic production or consumption'.[15] As with all the general exceptions, these measures must not constitute arbitrary or unjustifiable discrimination between countries, or disguised restrictions on international trade.

It is beyond the scope of this chapter to review legal actions brought before the WTO, but suffice it to say that the tendency is to interpret these exceptions narrowly. Moreover, international negotiations and agreements on environmental issues which may affect trade, rather than unilateral policies and actions, are encouraged. But what about the overall stance of the WTO regarding environmental issues? As early as 1971, a Group on Environmental Measures and International Trade was established by the GATT contracting parties. Interestingly enough, it never met. In 1991, with environmental issues finding a high profile on the international policy agenda, the Working Group was reactivated. Under the WTO, it was transformed into a Committee on Trade and the Environment, with a mandate to investigate the relationship between environmental and trade policies.[16] The preamble to the WTO also now recognizes the objective of sustainable development and the need to protect and preserve the environment. Indeed, more than one legal scholar has commented on the 'Greening of the GATT'.[17]

But, as might be expected, the WTO is coming under increasing pressure from environmental groups to act on the environmental degradation which spills over from one country to another, or is associated with trade-related production, consumption and transport, or which encourages a 'race to the bottom' in environmental standards as a means of securing comparative advantage. In October 1999, the WTO issued an important report on trade and the environment. It points out that: 'there is no basis for the sweeping generalizations that are often heard in the public debate, arguing that trade is either good for the environment, or bad for the environment. The real world of linkages are [*sic*] a little bit of both, or a shade of grey.'[18] The report seeks to answer a number of difficult questions. Is economic integration a threat to the environment? Does trade undermine the regulatory efforts of governments to control pollution and resource degradation? How can we ensure that economic growth driven by trade will help us to move towards a sustainable use of the world's environmental resources?

Not surprisingly, the general conclusion of the report is that trade liberalization reinforces the need for environmental co-operation. But it seems that the WTO sees its own role rather traditionally. One suggestion relates to addressing remaining trade barriers on environmental goods and services in order to reduce the costs of investing in clean production technologies and environmental management systems. Another is to seek reductions in government subsidies that harm the environment, including those in industries such as energy, agriculture and fishing.

To conclude, one approach which has been urged by a number of scholars is to expand the coverage of GATT Article XX to include a general exception for measures a country adopts to promote environmental objectives.[19] The challenge, of course, will be to ensure that this does not become a loophole allowing for trade discrimination or protectionism. In a broader sense, the co-operative model of the WTO, based on legal rights and obligations coupled with an effective dispute-settlement mechanism, could potentially serve as a model for a new global architecture of environmental co-operation.

4. Promotion of labour standards

The word 'labour' appears only once in the GATT, under Article XX for General Exceptions. It allows contracting parties to adopt measures 'relating to the products of prison labor'.[20] This type of provision is found in earlier trade agreements, and reflects national laws which ban the importation of goods produced by convict, forced and/or indentured labour. The moral motivation for such a provision is twofold: first, to shield the public from the consumption of 'tainted' goods, and second, to discourage prison production abroad. But there is also a competitive motivation, in that products of prison labour are likely to be less expensive because of reduced wage and social costs. Thus, there is an incentive for domestic industries to insist on the exclusion of such imports.

The larger labour issue which looms in the WTO context is that of the so-called 'social clause'. The underlying idea is to promote a set of internationally recognized workers' rights throughout the world. The exact composition of a core set of rights is subject to debate, but it would almost certainly include:[21]

(1) freedom of association, including the right to organize and bargain collectively;
(2) freedom from forced labour;
(3) a minimum age for child labour;
(4) certain minimum standards for working conditions (for example, safety and health standards, number of work hours and rest periods, elimination of employment discrimination).

At first glance, the adoption of a social clause appears to be a laudable objective. However, the next step would be to allow a country to impose duties against the imports of another country if they were produced in conditions which failed to meet these standards. This has been termed 'social dumping', and the procedures would operate along the lines described in the Polish golf cars example. As might be expected, the developing countries have strongly resisted such a move. They claim it would undermine their international competitive advantage, which is largely in labour costs. Moreover, given their lack of economic resources, many are simply unable to afford substantial improvements in working conditions. Finally, there is fear that a social clause could be invoked by richer countries as a means of protectionism, thereby closing off vital export markets.

The United States has been a leading proponent of a social clause for the WTO, but has been squarely blocked by other WTO members from putting the item on the trade agenda. To be sure, the WTO has affirmed its commitment to the observance of core labour standards, but insists that the competent body to deal with these issues is the International Labour Organization.[22]

5. Advancement of human rights

As might be anticipated from the treatment of labour standards under the WTO regime, there is no mention of human rights in the main trade agreement.[23] Given the enormous amount of effort the UN is devoting to the realization of civil and political rights, as well as economic, social and cultural rights, this may seem incongruous. Nonetheless, what about the use of trade leverage to advance the cause of human rights? This leads us to consider the question of economic sanctions, which have been defined as 'coercive economic measures taken against one or more foreign countries to force a change in policies, or at least to demonstrate a country's opinions about the other's policies'.[24]

The most prominent example in the human rights context, the major multilateral sanctions against South Africa, may be highlighted. Now, it must be understood that the WTO itself has no authority to impose economic sanctions for political reasons. Under Article XXI of the GATT, however, a member state may take action pursuant to its obligations under the United Nations Charter for the maintenance of international peace and security. The UN Charter outlines the circumstances under which the imposition of economic measures may be authorized, based on a Security Council determination of the existence of 'any threat to the peace, breach of the peace, or act of aggression'.[25] Violations of human rights are not readily deemed to constitute a threat to the peace. The situation in South Africa was exceptional in that the violence associated with apartheid posed a threat not only to the stability of the country itself, but to the whole region. Thus, far-reaching multilateral economic sanctions are rarely imposed to promote the value of human rights.

What about trade sanctions on a smaller scale? Countries may act unilaterally to restrict trade for national security or foreign policy reasons, and it can be argued that promoting human rights abroad is a legitimate foreign policy goal. Again, an example will illustrate some of the limitations of using trade restrictions to pressure another government to improve its human rights record. This one relates to threats by the USA to deny China its Most Favoured Nation (MFN) status. It should be borne in mind that this took place outside the GATT framework, as China is not a member of the GATT. Also, while suspending this tariff preference was a relatively limited threat, it would have had the effect of sharply reducing China's imports to the USA in a wide range of products.

What makes this example interesting is its specific human rights focus. After the massacre at Tiananmen Square in 1989, Bill Clinton, then campaigning for president, promised a 'get tough' policy on the Chinese. In 1993, the main tool for leverage came to be the withdrawal of MFN status should China fail to make improvements in certain areas of human rights.[26] 'Significant progress' was called for with respect to the following:

- taking steps to begin adhering to the Universal Declaration of Human Rights;
- releasing and providing an acceptable accounting for Chinese citizens imprisoned or detained for the non-violent expression of their political and religious beliefs, including such expression of beliefs in connection with the Democracy Wall and Tiananmen Square movements;
- ensuring humane treatment of prisoners, such as by allowing access to prisons by international humanitarian and human rights organizations;
- protecting Tibet's distinctive religious and cultural heritage; and
- permitting international radio and television broadcasts into China.

One year later, in May 1994, an evaluation of the Chinese record on human rights found no substantial progress. Nonetheless, in a reversal of policy, MFN treatment was extended and the new human rights requirements were abandoned.[27] The primary rationale was that increased economic contacts would better serve US interests and support human rights in China. Thus, there was an express de-linking of human rights from trade policy. It is fair to observe that there has been no serious attempt to revive this linkage.

Hans Küng, in *A Global Ethic for Global Politics and Economics*, faulted this reversal of US policy. He noted that the withdrawal of general idealistic demands for human rights due to pressure encourages the very type of political cynicism at home and abroad which was meant to be overcome.[28] As a footnote, we might echo one of the news commentators on the occasion of Chinese President Jiang Zemin's state visit to the UK in October 1999: have ethics been sacrificed for the sake of business deals?

Limitations on the use of trade law to promote non-economic values

A possible reaction to the foregoing discussion is the desire to urge sweeping changes in the trade law regime to protect this range of important values. Alleviation of poverty in the developing world, a clean environment, better working standards, greater observance of human rights – these enjoy widespread acceptance. But the question is not whether these values should be upheld, but *how*.

Five limitations might be noted in this regard. The first pertains to the resort to the law in general. All rules have a coercive element. At the international level, they also provoke difficult questions of sovereignty and interference in a country's domestic affairs. Perhaps other methods, such as diplomatic persuasion, voluntary codes of conduct or technical assistance may be viable alternatives in the pursuit of certain values.

Secondly, we must recognize that there is a diversity of values among nations and cultures. Indeed, preserving cultural diversity is one of the moral challenges of globalization. Areas of co-operation in solving common problems must be identified and promoted. At the same time, the imposition of values, especially by politically and economically powerful nations, must be guarded against.

Thirdly, even if it is appropriate to further certain values through domestic or international law, it may not be appropriate to do so through international trade law. Most trade experts insist that trade law should not be used to promote non-economic values. For example, one book urges that 'Attempts – whether unilateral or in the context of the WTO – to extend the reach of the concept of unfair trade to include differences in environmental or labour standards should be vigorously resisted.'[29] Another major study, which questions the harmonization of laws as a 'fair trade' prerequisite of 'free trade', argues that all such protectionist actions have the implicit if not explicit objective of maintaining employment in non-competitive industries.[30]

Fourth, there is a question of institutional competence. Trade officials, including those in the WTO secretariat, point out that the WTO has no expertise to judge complex matters related to social values. They are adamant that efforts to link these issues to the WTO regime would be divisive and counter-productive, eventually weakening the multilateral trading system and the benefits which flow from it.

Finally, a caution is in order against any unilateral resort to trade restrictions, even in an avowedly good cause, which runs afoul of the WTO regime. The importance of 'rule of law' is a global value which is increasingly emphasized in a variety of political and commercial contexts. To act outside the law undermines this value.

This need to assess actions on behalf of one social value in light of the possible impairment of another value leads us to a further set of cautions. Here, the concern pertains to the use of trade sanctions and similar measures for the advancement of human rights or other non-economic objectives. First of all, the usefulness of economic sanctions is debatable. As Philip Alston concludes in one study, 'The effectiveness of trade sanctions as a means by which to punish or to compel compliance with international legal norms has been questioned by the vast majority of writers who have analyzed the issue.'[31] This casts doubt on the validity of their use for both practical and ethical reasons. A second caution relates to the justification of the use of coercion. By definition, some degree of coercion is a feature of economic sanctions. As one writer put it, 'Economic sanctions are a species of warfare. To invert Clausewitz's famous aphorism, they are in a very real sense war – war by other means.'[32]

Thirdly, economic sanctions depend on the infliction of harm. The underlying logic of sanctions is to exact as much harm as possible to generate as much persuasive pressure as possible. The negative consequences in the target country can include loss of jobs, higher consumer prices, economic stagnation and, in the extreme, impoverishment and ill health. A great moral concern is the suffering they cause innocent individuals. Sanctions can also readily escalate into retaliation and 'trade wars', even drawing in other countries, leading to further economic difficulties and threats to international stability. All of this seems particularly disturbing if sanctions are imposed for the promotion of human rights, where the very people one is trying to help are likely to suffer.

Finally, it is appropriate to consider the contention that the link between trade and values, as understood in contemporary policy, is completely inverted. The expansion of trade, not the restriction of it, will best serve human rights and other non-economic objectives. Trade promotes interdependence and stimulates shared values. Greater interchange will open societies, diminish suspicion and promote mutual understanding. Taking this a step further, trade is seen to provide support for advocates of economic and political reform. Within more democratic systems, popular concerns about social values – the environment, labour, human rights – can readily be expressed and acted upon.

Prospects for a new round of trade negotiations

In late November of 1999, WTO ministers met in Seattle, WA, intending to launch major new negotiations further to liberalize trade and review trade rules in a variety of areas. In anticipation of this so-called Millennium Round, WTO members had proposed more than 150 possible topics for discussion, ranging from electronic commerce to fisheries to capacity-building.[33] But the finer points of agenda-setting were overshadowed by newspaper headlines proclaiming that a 'Storm Awaits World Trade Talks: Opposition is Growing in the Run-up to Seattle Negotiations.'[34]

As the meeting convened, tens of thousands of protesters from consumer, labour, environmental and other advocacy groups converged on the city. The massive external disruption, in addition to internal policy differences, scuppered any prospect for an agreement.[35] Subsequent street violence, property destruction and arrests captured media attention around the world, making the WTO a lightning rod for anti-globalization sentiment in general. WTO opponents have accused the trade body of favouring corporate freedom and profits over issues such as environmental protection and labour rights. But WTO defenders have argued that the system has helped international trade grow by 37 per cent between 1994 and 1998, creating jobs and prosperity for hundreds of millions of people worldwide.

The debate – and further well-organized protests at international meetings such as those of the World Bank, the G-7, and the World Economic Forum – has continued. The 'Battle of Seattle' has become a catchphrase for this antagonistic climate.

So how might a further round of trade talks take shape in this climate? The next WTO Ministerial Conference is scheduled to take place in Qatar in November 2001. Intensive and difficult preparations are currently under way.[36] The director-general of the WTO, New Zealander Mike Moore, is expecting the Qatar meeting successfully to launch a series of negotiations. The range of topics and the overall timing and scope of the talks are still unsettled. Nonetheless, it is clear that Moore hopes the WTO will address certain issues of fairness.[37] For example, he has urged that the less developed countries be granted greater market access and technical assistance. He recently observed:

> The overriding challenge today for the multilateral trading system, as a part of the global economy, is to join in international efforts to alleviate poverty, and to meet the internationally agreed targets of halving poverty by 2015. No challenge is greater. I see this as a moral issue as well. How can we deny opportunity for the most vulnerable of us and say that we are a fair rule-based system?[38]

In conclusion, the controversy surrounding the World Trade Organization must be seen in the broader context of public concern over the negative consequences of globalization. As political, commercial and personal interactions both intensify and accelerate, linkages between trade and values will continue to proliferate. Part of the tension arises from the fact that the existing system of trade rules is designed for the objective of trade liberalization and the benefits, both economic and non-economic, which flow from it. Such a system has provided little room for the articulation and advancement of non-economic values in a direct sense. It has also failed to take adequately into account how trade liberalization may impair certain values. This said, it seems likely that the 'Battle of Seattle' has just begun. Global economic institutions will come under ever greater pressure to play a positive role in assisting developing countries, preserving the environment, promoting labour standards and advancing human rights. In short, the pursuit of values in international trade will be a prominent feature of the culture of economics in the new millennium.

Notes

1 US Department of the Treasury, Final Determination of sales at less than fair value of electric golf cars from Poland; 40 Federal Register 25497, 11 June 1975. US International Trade Commission Investigation No. AA1921-147 (Pub. 740), 16 September 1975. The finding of dumping was revoked by the Department of Commerce due to changed circumstances on 8 August 1980; 45 Federal Register 52780. The Antidumping Act of 1921, as amended, is found in Title 19 of the US Code, Section 160ff.

2 These headlines are adapted from news coverage over the past four

years in publications such as *The Times*, *The Financial Times*, *The Economist*, *International Herald Tribune*, *New York Times* and *Time Magazine*.

[3] Insights on Christian perspectives can be found in a number of Hans Küng's books on global ethics, including *A Global Ethic for Global Politics and Economics* (London, 1997). Other helpful general works include Stephen Charles Mott, *A Christian Perspective on Political Thought* (New York, 1993) and Philip J. Wogaman, *Christian Perspectives on Politics* (London, 1988).

[4] General Agreement on Tariffs and Trade, 30 October 1947, *United Nations Treaty Service*, 55 (1947), 188. Useful texts on the subject which include a historical perspective are John H. Jackson, *The World Trading System: Law and Policy of International Economic Relations* (Cambridge, MA, 1997) and Robert E. Hudec, *The GATT Legal System and World Trade Diplomacy*, 2nd edn (Salem, NH, 1990).

[5] The Final Act Embodying the Results of the Uruguay Round of Multilateral Trade Negotiations, GATT Doc. MTN/FA Part I, reprinted in *International Legal Materials*, 33 (1994), was signed in Marrakesh on 15 December 1993, and includes the charter for the World Trade Organization and a series of related trade agreements, understandings and interpretations. John H. Jackson has prepared a helpful documentary supplement which contains key texts.

[6] '10 Benefits of the WTO Trading System', WTO website, 14 October 1999, *www.wto.org*.

[7] As Philip M. Nichols maintains, 'The World Trade Organization system, as currently envisioned, fails to take into account the fundamental nature of societal values, and creates little or no space in which such laws can exist' ('Trade without values', *Northwestern University Law Review*, 90/2 [1996], 658, 660).

[8] GATT, see above n. 4, art. XX(a). An excellent article on the subject is Steve Charnovitz, 'The moral exception in trade policy', *Virginia Journal of International Law*, 38 (1998), 689.

[9] The GATT protocol to introduce Part IV on Trade and Development dates from 8 February 1965; the Generalized System of Preferences was adopted on 25 June 1971. Commentary on the developing countries' use of legal procedures to restructure their positions in international trade is found in 'Developing countries and multilateral trade agreements: law and the promise of development', *Harvard Law Review*, 108 (1995), 1715.

[10] Discussion and summary charts on the developing countries' role in the WTO can be found in Bernard Hoekman and Michael Kostecki, *The Political Economy of the World Trading System: From GATT to WTO* (Oxford, 1998).

[11] Ibid.

[12] UNDP, *Human Development Report* (Geneva, 1998), 2. Further information can be found at the website: *www.undp.org*.

[13] 'Helping the world's poorest', *The Economist* (14 August 1999), 20; see also related articles on pp. 11 and 63 of the same issue.

[14] Information on both these initiatives can be found on the WTO website. In addition, in September 1999, a Conference on Developing Countries' Interests in a Millennium Round was held in Geneva.

[15] GATT, see above, n. 4, art. XX(b) and art. XX(g).

[16] Hoekman and Kostecki, *Political Economy*, 259.

[17] See, for example, Kym Anderson and Richard Blackhurst (eds.), *The Greening of World Trade Issues* (New York, 1992).

[18] 'Trade liberalization reinforces need for environmental cooperation', WTO press release of 8 October 1999, referring to WTO Secretariat's Trade and Environment Report. For a reaction to the report, see 'Embracing greenery', *The Economist* (9 October 1999), 125–6.

[19] Such an approach is advocated, for example, by Philip M. Nichols, 'Trade without values' (see above, n. 7). For a discussion focusing on the limits of the WTO in both environmental and labour areas, see Halina Ward, 'Common but differentiated debates: environment, labour and the World Trade Organization', *International and Comparative Law Quarterly*, 45 (1996), 592.

[20] GATT, see above, n. 4, art. XX(e).

[21] Raj Bhala analyses these issues in 'Clarifying the trade–labor link', *Columbia Journal of Transnational Law*, 37/1 (1998), 11 and especially 29–40.

[22] This was made clear at the first WTO Ministerial Conference in Singapore in December 1996. Further information on the International Labour Organization may be found at the website: *www.ilo.org*.

[23] While there is no harmonized enforcement mechanism under the WTO, countries may impose human rights conditions in extending preferential trade benefits. The USA, for example, imposes human rights conditions in its programs for GSP and the Caribbean Basin Initiative.

[24] Barry E. Carter, *International Economic Sanctions* (Cambridge, 1988), 4.

[25] UN Charter, Art. 39.

[26] The White House, Executive Order 12850, Conditions for Renewal of Most Favored Nation Status for the People's Republic of China in 1994, 28 May 1993.

[27] The White House, Office of the Press Secretary, press conference of 26 May 1994, regarding decisions on US policy towards China.

[28] Küng, *A Global Ethic for Global Politics and Economics*, 87.

[29] Hoekman and Kostecki, *Political Economy*, 249.

[30] This is the thrust of the two-volume study by Jagdish Bhagwati and Robert E. Hudec (eds.), *Fair Trade and Harmonization* (Cambridge, 1996).

[31] Philip Alston, 'International trade as an instrument of positive human rights policy', *Human Rights Quarterly*, 4 (1982), 155, 168.

[32] John P. Giraudo, 'Waging economic warfare: the sanctions power under the Constitution', *New York University Journal of International Law and Politics*, 19 (1987), 935.

[33] In 1999, there was much speculation about likely topics for the proposed Millennium Round agenda, beyond the traditional GATT concerns such as tariff reduction. This was taken up by a group of experts at Templeton Management College shortly before the Seattle meeting. In addition to agriculture, services and developing country concerns, items such as textiles, e-commerce, enforcement, government procurement and trade facilitation were mentioned as top issues. The group also indicated what was likely to be at the bottom of the agenda: labour rights, environmental questions and competition. Research Workshop on the WTO Millennium Round: Issues and Influences, Templeton Management College, Oxford University, 18 October 1999.

[34] *The International Herald Tribune*, 3 November 1999, 11, also observed that 'the 135-nation WTO, and the global open-trading system it stands for, are facing their greatest challenge since the organization was founded . . .'

[35] See the *Newsweek* cover story, 'The Battle of Seattle', 13 December 1999. In addition to the riots, several substantive issues contributed to the failure of the ministerial meeting. One was the US administration's desire to use the WTO to raise labour standards, which provoked developing countries' suspicions about protectionism. Another was EU resistance to agricultural policy reform.

[36] See the WTO website for the latest status on the prospects for a trade round. Also note that according to agreements reached during the Uruguay Round, new negotiations in the area of services and agriculture were mandated to begin in the year 2000 and are currently under way.

[37] This attitude was clear from the outset of Moore's term. In 1999, he spelled out his priorities for the outcome of the Seattle ministerial. Significantly, he noted: 'It's a moral issue as well. A world now exists polarized by poverty and opportunity as it was once polarized by the cold war. I will judge my term in office by how much we could improve the conditions and opportunities for the most vulnerable

economies.' 'Moore spells out priorities for Seattle Ministerial Conference', WTO press release, 2 September 1999.

[38] Text of video message by Mr Mike Moore, Director-General, at the WTO/FORSEC Trade Policy Course for Pacific Island Countries, Fiji, 5–9 March, 2001. Available on WTO website, news items.

7

Work and unemployment

ANDREW HENLEY

Introduction

Work occupies the majority of the adult population for around half of their waking hours. It occupies them for perhaps two-thirds of the days of the year. Participation in the labour market is an activity that involves, according to the 1999 Labour Force Survey, 27.4 million Britons. Nearly four-fifths of the population who are between sixteen and state retirement age are either in work or looking for it ('economically active'). It will therefore come as no surprise that economists expend considerable effort in analysing and investigating the labour market. The labour market is prone to failure, just as and perhaps more so than any other market. The most obvious symptom of this failure is unemployment. It is perhaps no understatement to describe unemployment as the most persistent and pressing economic problem within the industrialized world over the last century, a few years of world war and a short and exceptional period after the Second World War apart. According to the internationally recognized definition used by the International Labour Office, unemployment in the UK stood in spring 1999 at a little over 6 per cent of the total workforce. This is a rate that is low by comparison with the experience of the previous twenty years. Elsewhere in Europe the picture is much worse – France, Germany, Italy and Spain all have substantially higher and stubbornly higher rates (the EU average in June 1999 stood at 9.4 per cent). In Japan unemployment is rising rapidly. The USA, with unemployment at 4.3 per cent, currently enjoys the best performance of the major, large industrialized economies of the world. If accurate unemployment statistics were available for the former communist states of the Soviet bloc they would reveal a very dismal state of affairs indeed.

In this chapter I wish to examine, from an academic economist's perspective, the biblical perspective on work and the directions in which that has informed Christian social ethical teaching. I will then attempt to summarize the state of mainstream economic analysis on the labour market and offer a critical perspective on it. This will allow me to identify and discuss what I think are the key themes in current, secular economic analysis of work and employment, and to appraise these from a Christian perspective. In turn I will offer some conclusions about the important issues for Christian socio-economic thinking at the turn of the third Christian millennium.

The biblical context

Have Christian economists anything distinctive to say on the subject of work and unemployment? One point of view might be that the kind of society portrayed in the Bible (and in particular in the Old Testament) was a tribally organized, agrarian one in which the phenomenon of unemployment does not arise. Furthermore, the organization of work within that society was so far removed from contemporary experience of an industrial and post-industrial world that the biblical material provides virtually nothing that we can meaningfully apply. At the other extreme is a perspective that takes a highly literal approach to the biblical material. This might suggest, for example, that any Christian inquiry into the nature of public policy towards the labour market should be tightly circumscribed by the observation that Jewish society in biblical times displayed no forms of state-provided welfare or social insurance.

Somewhere between these extremes is a position adopted by many contemporary Christian economists to greater or lesser extent. This position tries to establish Christian social ethical principles from which a Christian understanding of and prescription for contemporary socio-economic concerns can be approached. What is the biblical context within which those principles might rest? Beginning with the Old Testament and with the account of the relationship between God, his chosen people and the Promised Land, it is possible to argue that we find a model or paradigm of economic and social relationships. These are the relationships that God intends should exist between himself, humankind and the earthly resources that are the outcome of his providence. The regulations contained within the Pentateuch in particular govern those economic interrelationships that God intended should operate amongst his chosen Israelite nation, in their collective stewardship of those resources and their work to use those resources to sustain themselves, both physically and spiritually.

The establishment of a covenantal relationship between God and the Jewish people is at the foundation of this socio-economic model. The partial fulfilment of this covenant is reached with the return of the children of Israel to the Promised Land. The model or ideal-type for their relationship with God and with that land is laid out in particular in the material contained within Exodus 20: 22–23: 19, and in Leviticus, especially in chapter 25 with the institution of the Jubilee, and throughout Deuteronomy, but especially in chapters 15, 19 and 26. Even prior to the Fall, it is apparent that men and women have a co-operative labouring enterprise to perform in caring for the created order (Genesis 2: 15). This is implicitly re-emphasized within the Mosaic regulations, although in a corrupted post-Fall world work, which may be rewarding, will also be hard and burdensome.

The economic dimension (humankind's work in stewardship of creation) can only be understood within the context of the balancing relationships of God's sovereign ownership of the economic world and humankind's spiritual relationship with God, as creatures in his own image.[1] It hardly needs to be stated that this represents a contextualization of economic life that does not attract discussion in the mainstream economics literature. These relationships can be extended paradigmatically to highlight under the New Covenant the balance that exists between God, his church and the wider resources of his blessing. The Christian commission to work to advance God's kingdom can be seen as applying as much in economic terms as in spiritual ones. In the New Testament, Jesus' concern for the social and economic, as well as the spiritual, is clearly to be found. One of the strongest symbols of this is perhaps the Nazareth manifesto in Luke 4. Here Jesus announces 'good news for the poor' and 'release for the oppressed' (4: 18) in the context of a general proclamation of the 'year of the Lord's favour'. The socio-economic symbolism here is in the direct reference to the Levitical jubiliary provisions, making clear that Jesus is referring to an economic and social fulfilment, as well as a spiritual one.[2] One reservation might be that this proclamation is solely concerned with eschatology, a 'counsel of perfection' which gives a taste of the perfect economic and social relationships that will exist in the future, redeemed world after the return of Christ. But this objection seems based on a highly incomplete picture of Jesus' teaching and ministry, a ministry that time and again challenged directly the contemporary social and economic order.

Some Christian economists place their strongest emphasis on the implications for the organization of economic activity implied within the parables, such as that of the talents (Matthew 25: 14–30; Luke 19: 11–27). From these they draw conclusions about employee and employer responsibilities, wealth creation and the distribution of the rewards of labour.

The challenge for the economist who is also a Christian is to overcome the enormous hermeneutic task entailed in applying the principles contained within the corpus of biblical material to contemporary society. The challenge is perhaps no different from that faced by any other interpreter of scripture, except that the problem is made more acute by the ideologically charged nature of contemporary economic methodology. Compare for example the possible warnings against labouring to accumulate contained within the parable of the rich fool (Luke 12: 31–21) or within the Sermon on the Mount (Matthew 6: 19–24) with the praise bestowed on those servants who invest wisely as described in the parable of the talents. There are enormous possibilities here for the economist to start from a predetermined ideological position and to quote scripture selectively in support. Consequently, the task of establishing derived social principles for the contemporary world is not straightforward. Nevertheless, turning to specific questions to do with the labour market, there is probably a broad measure of agreement about the theological context of work. Where there is disagreement, it is over how that theological context ought to be applied in terms of specific analyses and policies.

Towards a theology of work

Humankind's role as stewards of creation is fundamental to a theological understanding of men's and women's relationship with God. The idea of stewardship entails a function of husbandry of scarce and valuable resources. It also implies an employment function. Work therefore has a central theological dimension within a Christian perspective. It is part of our self-fulfilment, in that self-fulfilment from a Christian point of view comes through the understanding and enjoyment of a relationship with God, made possible through the redemptive work of Christ. Contrast this with classical Greco-Roman ideas that work was a sordid activity from which the higher orders in society should refrain in favour of artistic and intellectual pursuit. The pervasive nature of this attitude over the last two millennia of European society has been pronounced. Occasionally it has provoked social revolution. At the opposite extreme of this is a tendency to deify work, in the sense that it becomes an individual's *raison d'être*. Calvin saw work as 'calling'; an idea taken up with a vengeance in Protestant Puritan thinking about 'vocation' and 'duty'.[3] 'Time is short and work is long,' preached the Puritan Richard Baxter.[4] If one subscribes to the Weberian thesis, then this was critical to the development of industrial capitalist economies.[5]

Modern 'neo-classical' economics is largely, of course, the methodological product of Enlightenment thinking in the eighteenth century. Adam Smith, as a Deist, viewed the physical world as self-regulated, set in train by a distant Creator. The socio-economic world could emulate this, through the *laissez-faire* principles of the self-regulating economy.[6] As Norman Hampson put it, Smith's ideas seemed to eliminate the traditional Christian conflict between virtue (work as an end in itself) and acquisitiveness (work as a means to the end of personal economic betterment) while retaining a belief in the providence of God.[7]

Returning to a Christian perspective, I have already highlighted the importance of work to the theological integrity of human existence, the stewardship function and the need to place work within the 'relational' or social context. Those Christian economists and social ethicists who attempt to steer what I described earlier as a middle way between the irrelevance and the literal application of biblical material tend to summarize these aspects of economic life within their statements of Christian social principles.[8] Donald Hay's following three statements[9] are both comprehensive and to the point:

(1) People have a right and an obligation to work.
(2) Work is a means of exercising stewardship.
(3) Work is a social activity in which people co-operate as individual stewards of individual talents and as joint stewards of resources.

So, to the Christian, work is necessary to retain the relational balance between a loving God, humankind and creation. Work is a creation provision, reflecting the nature of God and predating the Fall. It is part of the natural rhythm of men and women (Psalm 104: 23) and their self-fulfilment. Despite the Fall, work remains essential to human dignity. To that end men and women ought to have access to, and delegated control over, those resources necessary to exercise good stewardship. In the exercise of this stewardship employment should as far as possible take the form of co-operation in a common enterprise. The corollary here is that unemployment leads, in William Temple's words, to 'moral isolation'.[10] For the Christian the maintenance of full employment (broadly defined to include unpaid work in the home and voluntary service as well as paid formal employment) ought to be a reasonable goal. To summarize: work is not an end itself, nor is it solely a means to the end of material production and consumption. Rather, it ought to be seen as a means to support and sustain life and to support and sustain others.

Contemporary economic analysis of work and unemployment

How does the economist's textbook analysis of the labour market, rooted in post-Enlightenment methodological individualism, square up to this understanding of work? The typical textbook, at least in the first half a dozen chapters, will attempt to define something called the 'market for labour' in which overall wage and employment levels are determined by the interaction of supply (derived from individual worker-consumers) and demand (derived from employers, usually firms). This market operates in much the same way as for any other commodity or service, be that baked beans, haircuts or Treasury bills (see Figure 7.1).

A Marshallian or Walrasian adjustment mechanism regulates the market through respectively either price or quantity adjustment to establish an equilibrium wage and level of employment. A high wage encourages labour supply, a low wage discourages it. In equilibrium any unemployment is 'voluntary' in the sense that those without jobs are so because they choose not to work at the wage on offer (shown by the distance marked by the arrows in Figure 7.1). If unemployment is 'involuntary', then it is because of market inflexibility or failure. In this case, market failure results in the unemployed receiving no job offers, and so not having the opportunity to accept or turn down a particular wage level. Behind the labour supply relationship is an essentially static, individualistic model of behaviour, with a rather classical view of

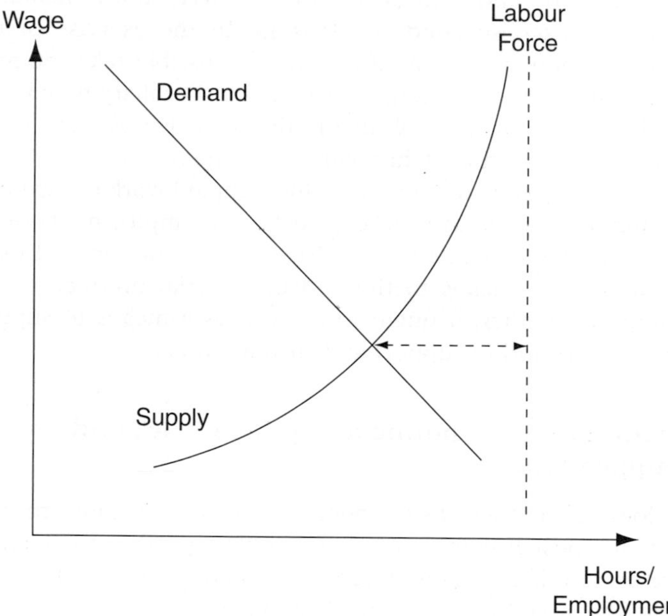

Equilibrium wage and employment are given by the intersection of the labour demand and labour supply schedules. The distance between this level of employment and the total labour force identifies the extent of voluntary employment.

Figure 7.1 The neo-classical labour market

work as 'not leisure'. This is a world in which work is an 'evil' necessary to generate the wherewithal to purchase desirable goods and services. Labour supply is therefore derived from the relative attractiveness of material goods or services and leisure. It is rarely acknowledged that these two might be complementary. The worker's choice is constrained by income resources derived from unearned sources such as personal wealth or state welfare, and by the prevailing rate of pay of any job offers (see Figure 7.2).

The labour demand curve is derived using neo-classical economic principles from a model of a profit-maximizing (or cost-minimizing) firm. In effect, the firm demands a 'flow' of labour services or effort from a 'stock' of employees. In the

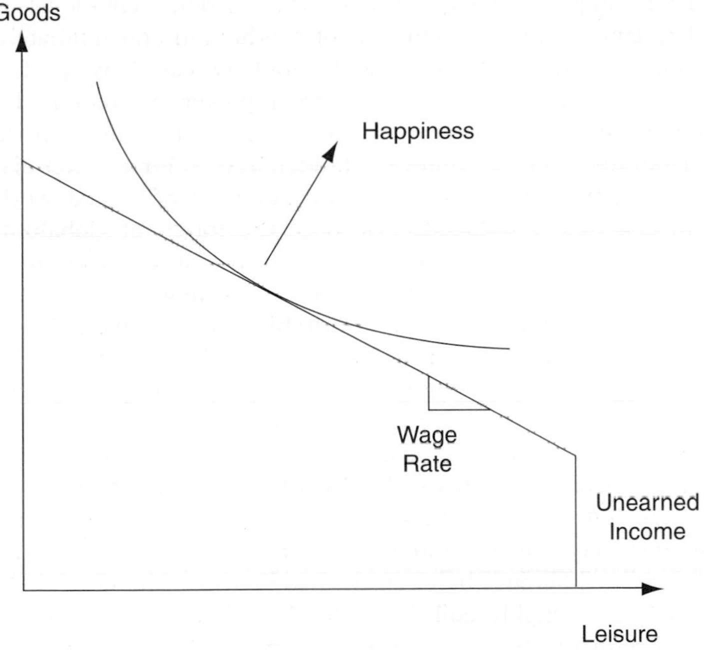

The curved schedule maps out a locus of 'indifference' between different combinations of goods and leisure. Less of one means more of the other at a diminishing rate. The worker's budget constraint is fixed by the wage on offer and any unearned income available. The point where the indifference curve is tangential to the budget constraint gives the worker's optimal combination of goods and leisure. Once leisure is defined (and assuming hours of sleep is a fixed constant) then hours of work are given by what is left of the day.

Figure 7.2 The goods–leisure trade-off and labour supply

simplest model, that stock is infinitely divisible and costlessly and instantaneously alterable. In more complex analyses the firm may be able to invest in resources to improve the quality of that stock through education and training – so-called 'human capital' investment. Capital equipment and labour are also typically assumed to be infinitely substitutable one for another, at least over the longer run. However, the representation of technology, as typically assumed, incorporates diminishing marginal gain from adding additional workers to a *given* stock of capital equipment. If the wage rate rises the firm can afford fewer workers, *given* capital, for the same cost budget and so can produce less. Over the longer run it may substitute towards capital and away from labour.

This brings us to the question of whether new technologies lead to less labour-intensive methods of production and ultimately to unemployment. Certainly new technology can have profound effects on the balance of skills that an employer may require. Low-skilled workers in Britain on the verge of the third Christian millennium face a double disadvantage. First, skill-biased technological change raises the productivity of skilled workers relative to the less skilled.[11] Second, the forces of globalization reduce the demand for low-skilled British workers who are very expensive relative to similar workers in the newly industrializing world. But to argue that this inevitably leads to unemployment misunderstands the broader picture. Labour-saving innovation can, under conditions of macroeconomic stability, lead, either through export growth or through efficiency gains at home, to growth in the domestic economy. New so-called 'endogenous' growth theories point to the possibility of a virtuous circle between human capital accumulation, research and development into new technologies and higher real incomes. On the supply side, as the difference between the productivity (therefore the rate of pay) of the highly skilled and the low-skilled grows wider, the rate of return to education and training increases and encourages those with the wrong skills or none at all to acquire new skills. The problem is that this process is far from instantaneous. Lags and adjustment costs mean that things may get worse before they get better.

The analysis presented so far assumes atomistic, individualistic workers and firms, with no attention paid to the idea that work ought to be a co-operative activity. In the UK nearly two-fifths of the labour force are still members of a trade union, despite declining union membership over the last twenty years. (In some European countries, such as in Scandinavia, this figure is as high as four-fifths, although in the USA it is only one-fifth.) Perhaps two-thirds of British workers have their pay and conditions of employment established through collective negotiation. How does economics address this? The mainstream approach is to replace the utilitarian materialist individual with a utilitarian materialist trade union that optimally trades off higher wages against fewer members.

Not surprisingly this leads to a very pessimistic view of collective organization in the workplace. Unions, if they possess significant bargaining strength, drive up wages and displace workers into other jobs for which they may be overqualified, or at worst into unemployment. Some economists attribute the rise in unemployment during the 1970s and 1980s almost exclusively to excessively powerful trade unions.[12] However, theorizing in this vein leaves no room for approaching such collective organizations as social, relational entities with the potential to exercise a beneficial representative function in the workplace as well as the potential to disrupt. There is a substantial tradition within Christian and particularly Catholic social teaching for a model of collective representation that works for social cohesion and the good of the whole.[13] In the UK we may have seen rather more of the disruptive role than the cohesive one, but that should not preclude a methodological approach which encompasses both roles.

So in order to investigate the kind of issues in which secular labour economists are interested, these economists have abstracted away much of the complexity of actual employment relationships. For the Christian economist there are two important issues to address. The first is whether, in this analysis, the richness of the Christian perspective on work has been assumed away. The second is whether the issues in which secular labour economists are interested, and for which they have developed a rather abstracted model of reality, are the appropriate ones.

Themes in contemporary labour economics

The picture presented in the previous paragraphs was deliberately stylized. It illustrates the point of departure for the academic treatment of the complex issues of wage and employment determination. I now want to outline some of the themes emerging from the contemporary corpus of academic research in labour economics.

Incentives and motivation

As we have seen, the textbook model assumes that individual workers and employers are motivated by self-interest. As with all theories of economic behaviour, this presents the economist with a tension between a description of economic behaviour that may for the most part be accurate in the real world and a desire to encompass how agents ought to behave. This said, recent concerns of labour economists have been rather less fundamental. One issue is whether workers alter their behaviour if they are paid more and what might be the consequences of this. Leading on from this is the question of why in practice employers are reluctant to cut wages when economic theory suggests that it would be rational to do so.[14] A second issue concerns whether workers are motivated by concerns beyond simply higher current earnings, and if they are, what might the consequences be.

Efficiency wage theory proposes a positive relationship between effort and wages.[15] There are a number of explanations for this. One particularly pessimistic model is that of Carl Shapiro and Joseph Stiglitz who suggest that higher wages reduce the extent to which workers 'shirk' on the job because they have more to lose if they are caught and get fired.[16] This model gives a prediction that is remarkably similar to the Marxian explanation of why capitalist economies need a 'reserve army' of the unemployed – a certain level of unemployment is necessary to discipline the employed into not shirking. A rather more attractive explanation for the same phenomenon is to be found in George Akerlof's 'gift-exchange' model: workers give higher effort on the job, above what is strictly necessary to keep them employed, because their employer is prepared to pay higher wages.[17] The link with the question of downward wage flexibility is that theories such as these can be used as explanations as to why employers do not seem to cut wages in response to an excess supply of labour, but I shall return to this below.

If workers have the luxury of a choice, it is the whole remuneration and conditions package a job offers, and not just its current earnings, that will attract them. The growth of performance- and profit-related pay schemes has led economists to ask whether such incentive systems enhance productivity, because they might bring about a congruency of interest between employee and employer. Theoretical results establish that 'incentive-compatible' employment contracts, with an appropriate mix of flat-rate and performance-related pay elements, will overcome the 'principal-agent' problem, which arises because employers cannot continually and perfectly monitor employee effort (the 'asymmetric information' problem). Some such as Martin Weitzman of Harvard University go further and suggest that the 'share economy' would enjoy improved levels of inflation and unemployment compared to one based solely on flat-rate wage payments.[18] The evidence for such beneficial effects is far from compelling, suggesting either that workers are not motivated at all by bonus payments, or that such bonus payments are too small and attenuated through overall group performance to make any difference. A third possibility is that such schemes become all too rapidly 'institutionalized', and thus ineffective.

One further area of considerable interest within the overall theme of incentives concerns the degree of motivation that those who are unemployed have to search for jobs. Are the unemployed solely motivated by a comparison of the pecuniary rewards of remaining unemployed relative to finding work, or are other non-pecuniary concerns important? Once again, one would like to think that the unemployed would prefer to work whatever the relative rewards from staying on the dole, but empirical human nature points to the existence of 'disincentive' effects. (Some 'disincentive' effects arise because of tax-induced poverty traps and point to failures in tax systems.) How big are such effects? The consensus answer is that they are significant, though perhaps not too large. British estimates suggest that a 10 per cent increase in the generosity of unemployment benefits might lead to a 5 per cent reduction in the escape probability from unemployment.[19] A further issue concerns whether workers become demotivated in their search for a job as their unemployment duration rises and so are less likely to escape unemployment as time passes ('duration dependence'). If overgenerous unemployment benefits reduce the initial escape probability, then as time passes they could become the driving force of long-term unemployment. Evidence suggests that this is unlikely to be the case, implying that long-term unemployment is more likely to be the result of skill erosion.[20]

Flexibility

Why does the price of labour, unlike, for example, the price of tomatoes, appear only imperfectly to adjust to an excess supply in the market? It was Keynes who first focused on the impossibility of wage flexibility operating to cure unemployment.[21] In doing so he highlighted the difference between two competing types of explanation for unemployment. The first assumes that workers are unemployed because they do not wish to accept the jobs on offer at the prevailing wage. The second focuses on market imperfections that prevent the unemployed from receiving job offers at any wage level. However, Keynes failed to provide a convincing explanation for why firms do not cut wages sufficiently in recessions. There has been a lot of effort directed towards this question in the last fifteen years (the so-called New-Keynesian approach). Truman F. Bewley, on the basis of survey evidence conducted in American firms, suggests that employers do not cut wages when the business cycle falls because of the fear that pay cuts 'express hostility to the workforce' and may be interpreted as 'an insult'.[22] This suggests that moral norms such as fairness and reciprocity may be important influences on wage determination and therefore on the ability of the labour market to adjust to clear unemployment.[23] The efficiency wage idea, already discussed, is one possible explanation since it suggests that firms fear damaging effects on productivity if they cut wages. Other economists have pointed to the existence of 'implicit contracts' which lock workers and employers into contracts of employment that may be inappropriate if unexpectedly adverse economic outcomes occur. A further explanation is to be found in the behaviour of trade unions, who may be reluctant to bargain pay concessions to preserve jobs. This is because, at the average, their memberships may care little about job losses since the newest recruits are usually the ones to be fired first. They may care even less about the unemployed who are altogether outside the workplace. Such models are known as insider–outsider models.[24] They can generate the alarming prediction that once an adverse economic shock has generated a rise in the jobless total, unemployment will have no tendency to return to its previous level – the phenomenon of path dependency. Such an effect is known by the term 'hysteresis', borrowed from physics.[25] Many economists have gravitated towards this idea as an explanation for the persistently high level of unemployment in many European economies.

One of the conclusions to emerge from such ideas is that the costs of the labour-market actions of one group may be borne by others. Consequently, a greater sense of cohesion between labour-market participants may reap benefits for all, and go some way to responding to Hay's principle 3 above. Investigation of the rather superior performance of some of the smaller, particularly Scandinavian, economies during the 1970s and 1980s suggests that they managed largely to avoid hysteresis and long-term unemployment problems. It is often proposed that this was through a greater degree of cohesion in pay-setting and consensus-forming activity about what 'the economy could afford to pay'.[26] However, questions about economic performance in Scandinavia since 1990 and the fiscal costs of such a system raise enormous doubts about the international transferability of the so-called Swedish model.

Even the most cursory reading of the relevant literature would lead the observer to think that labour 'flexibility' was unambiguously 'a good thing'. I am far from sure that economists should be so sanguine. They should take a wider view of personal and social costs of flexibility, particularly where these might undermine social cohesion.

Earnings structure, discrimination and inequality

In the neo-classical economic paradigm, wages are a return to the productivity of labour. Where productivity is high and wages are high, labour supply will respond. One of the core predictions of the model is that wage rates across different groups of workers, such as between industries, occupations or regions, ought by market forces to be equalized net of any non-pecuniary advantages. Discussion of the sources of such advantages can be traced back to Adam Smith. However, much evidence suggests that the forces of equalization are weak. For example, the UK New Earnings

Survey reveals that between 1975 and 1993 the ratio of female to male basic earnings only moved from 0.58 to 0.65.[27] There are various explanations for this, most of which hinge on some market failure which prevents different groups of workers from competing with others. Some of these abandon the competitive model entirely in favour of more institutionalist approaches.[28] One source of such pay differences is of course discrimination. Nobel Laureate Gary Becker's well-known neo-classical treatment[29] rests on employers possessing a 'taste' for discrimination. This results in their being prepared to sacrifice profit in order not to have workers with a given characteristic in their employ, even though those workers might potentially be better at the job. But such discrimination ought to be competed away by more profitable employers who choose not to discriminate. An alternative explanation highlights the difficulties and costs an employer faces in identifying the true productivity of individual workers. 'Statistical' discrimination occurs when employers exclude on the basis of some characteristic because on average workers with that characteristic are less productive.

One consequence of discrimination is that workers can become segmented – for example, female or black workers become grouped in more poorly paid, poorer-quality jobs. Indeed, one consequence of insider union-bargaining power in the skilled, white-male sector may be the creation of excess supply in outsider segments of the labour market. In the USA, where there is greater wage flexibility and less generous unemployment insurance, this has perhaps contributed to the growth of poor-quality, low-paid part-time employment. In Europe, where greater government regulation and more generous unemployment insurance apply, the consequence is more likely to have been stubbornly high rates of unemployment. Pre-tax wage inequality has been rising in countries such as the UK and USA since the late 1970s.[30] This has occurred in part for the reasons sketched above. The trend may also reflect rising individual returns to skills and education, leaving the untrained and uneducated unable to keep up. Whatever the explanation, the trend towards greater wage inequality is one that governments have apparently been unwilling or unable to reverse.

Labour economists who eschew the neo-classical market model in favour of radical or institutionalist explanations for wage and employment determination focus on the creation of 'internal' labour markets within firms and organizations as devices for maintaining employee loyalty to the company whilst creating competition between workers for promotion internally. A whole subdiscipline of 'personnel economics' has arisen to address these issues, offering economic-theoretic explanations for contemporary phenomena in human resource management practice.[31]

Regulation and government intervention in the labour market

What, if any, is the appropriate role for government? In the context of policies to alleviate unemployment, Dennis Snower points out that the kind of role that an economist will propose for government policy will depend on the particular theory of the labour market to which he or she subscribes.[32] We can go a stage further than this and say that the kind of theory about the operation of the labour market to which an economist subscribes will depend on the ideological preconceptions and value judgements which he or she brings to bear on his or her theorizing. A labour economist from a *laissez-faire* position will have a very different perspective on the world, both as it is and as it ought to be, from an institutionalist or a radical interventionist.

The demise of Keynesian demand management as an effective tool for influencing the aggregate employment level led from the late 1960s onwards to the growth in popularity of various forms of 'equilibrium' theories of unemployment. Milton Friedman popularized the idea of the natural rate of unemployment, more recently and perhaps more accurately entitled the non-accelerating inflation rate of unemployment (NAIRU). Friedman came to the conclusion that any government demand-side policy influence on the rate of unemployment was likely to be temporary and eventually would be obliterated by corresponding movements in labour supply. Even stronger forms of the theory suggested that agents in the economy would always correctly 'double-guess' any government attempts to influence the demand for labour – they would have 'rational expectations'. Consequently, demand management policy was futile. On first impression these ideas seem highly pessimistic – the economy was so self-regulating that no government could exercise any permanent influence. The only role for government in this world is to attempt to influence the supply-side-determined influences on the equilibrium unemployment level itself. This might be through reducing the generosity of unemployment benefits in order to lower the disincentive effect, or through reducing the power of trade unions to raise wages and restrict labour supply, or through removing regulations governing the scale of hiring and firing costs. New Keynesians would, in reply, question whether there is anything 'natural' or exogenous (that is determined from outside the system) about the equilibrium rate of unemployment. This brings us back to the possibility, discussed already, that the level of employment in the economy may be path-dependent.

So the end of the post-war Keynesian consensus has pushed economists away from viewing labour-market problems as solely problems of labour demand towards greater consideration of supply-side policies or a 'both blades of the scissors' approach. This has also had the effect of focusing policy in terms of microeconomic rather than macroeconomic factors. So, for example, one is now more likely to hear economists advocating the correction of market failures in the provision of retraining for the unemployed rather than aggregate demand management to boost national demand for labour. Furthermore, there is now something of a consensus emerging that the function of government is to undertake 'employment-replacement' or 'employment-enhancement' strategies rather than merely providing 'income-replacement' for the unemployed. There are some differences of nuance: some talk about the importance of 'active labour-market policies' and appeal to the success of Swedish or German labour-market policies; others talk of 'work-for-welfare' schemes and cite the need to overcome unemployment benefit disincentive effects and to increase competition between the employed and unemployed.

The issue of what is an appropriate level of government regulation of the employer–employee relationship is a particularly thorny one. Minimum wage legislation or EU-imposed minimum employment standards are easily criticized from within the purview of the simple neo-classical model of the labour market. They have the potential to prevent the market from equating demand with supply, at least at full employment, and thus lead to an excess supply of labour. The counter-argument is rather more complex. It is usually framed in terms of the need to correct some other market failure, such as the adverse selection problem through which employers with poor standards of employment are able to compete 'unfairly' on final product price and drive 'responsible' employers out of business.

Conclusion: Christian responses

As with any branch of economics, labour economists face a tension between a secular economics which treats economic agents as self-seeking (as a positivist generalization about the actual way in which people behave) and normative ethical ideals which concern the way agents ought to behave. The former may be a pretty accurate description of human behaviour; the latter from the Christian perspective would incorporate the biblical ideals to which Christians aspire. The tension becomes particularly acute when economists move from description to prescription. This follows from the ideological tension between the tradition that secular economics is a positive (that is, value-free) scientific pursuit, and the reality that economists who are Christians will want to make normative statements about economic activity on the basis of biblical principles.

So when labour economists examine how workers are motivated and what incentive structures may improve the operation of the labour market, they are working from models of worker and employer behaviour which are rooted in a pessimistic, materialist description of human nature. When they consider appropriate policy prescriptions to deal with labour-market failures, such as unemployment, then those prescriptions are deduced from the same modelling strategy. If the world of work and employment relationships is to be motivated by the biblical concern of stewardship, then ideas about selfless behaviour enter very explicitly. That selfless behaviour, as we have seen, is referential to God, a feature that cannot easily be enveloped within secular theory and models. The question, therefore, is just how pessimistic should economists be about human nature in the workplace? Of course, sin is pervasive and within that context individuals will inevitably be materialistically motivated. On the other hand, within every person (whether Christian or not) there is something of the image of God. Work is part of the divine nature and so for men and women work, be it paid or unpaid, has the capacity to enrich and give purpose to life. The secular economics tradition sees work in purely consequentialist terms, as merely the means to material ends. In this, secular economics has assumed away the richness of the Christian perspective on work.

Suppose we start by rejecting the neo-classical tradition which assumes that enlightened self-interest will lead to the greater good, as starting from the wrong description of human nature, and seek to incorporate something of how we think economic agents ought to behave. An important issue that arises for labour economists is whether the employment relationship can be made to work in such a way as to enhance the image of God in both employers and employees. To give one example, the principle that work is social activity in which people co-operate as stewards points to the desirability of employee involvement and consultation in decision-making. Recent work that points towards the importance of mutual reciprocity or co-operation as a feature of employment contracts may go some way in this direction. However, that reciprocity is seen as the outcome of rational self-interested behaviour in a 'repeated game' in which the parties learn to co-operate. It is not an expression of the outworking of an ethical ideal of mutuality.

Perhaps even more fundamentally, if we fail to address the importance of nurturing God's image in others, will we inadvertently undermine that image if we continue to work with models that explicitly incorporate the feature that agents respond to materialistic incentives? In a nutshell, this amounts to the familiar question of whether people are greedy in the economic sphere because that is human nature, or because economists tell them it is a good thing if they are. By and large, economists do not have any convincing answers to this paradox.

The idea of labour-market flexibility is troublesome for the Christian. This is because flexibility imposes costs as well as benefits, and those costs can undermine biblical ideas that work is a relational activity. Yes, economics does recognize that labour is a 'quasi-fixed' factor of production involving non-trivial recruitment, training and firing costs. But a cursory reading of much that has recently been written on labour-market flexibility gives the impression that the implicit solution to the problem of inefficient matching of workers to jobs is adopting policies that whittle away at those costs.

In the short term, the non-economic costs of labour flexibility become apparent as traffic congestion and long travel-to-work times. Over the longer term, these costs show up as children grow up away from their extended families and communities and as workplaces become places where relationships are transient and underdeveloped. Furthermore, 'internal labour markets' within organizations, which seek to motivate workers by offering career progression, can create an excessive level of interpersonal competition within organizations. This seems contrary to the ideal of work as a relational activity based on mutual co-operation in a shared stewarding endeavour.

Of course within the parables of the talents (Luke 19: 11–27) and of the workers in the vineyard (Matthew 20: 1–16) we seem to have a justification for managerial prerogative on pay and employment matters. The model of pay structure presented here is very odd indeed. It is highly problematic, if not downright misleading, to think that Jesus intended these parables to be applied beyond stories about the sovereignty of God in his kingdom and the responsibility he places on his stewards within that kingdom. Pay structures raise questions not only of motivation and incentive but also of justice. Employers ought to be seen to treat workers justly. This is balanced by a duty on the part of employees to behave responsibly towards others in the organization. What this means in practice in a modern industrial organization may be complicated to unravel, but it would certainly preclude forms of pay discrimination, or discrimination against some workers by others.

The issue of discrimination raises very important wider issues about economic justice which are rarely dealt with within the narrow confines of textbook theory. Workers who are discriminated against have a much reduced incentive to engage in education and training and so they appear to receive less pay largely because they are less qualified. Providing the means to allow individual workers (who might in fact be unemployed workers) to escape from such a trap would seem to be an important principle that a Christian approach might support. It accords with my understanding of the economic principle behind the Jubilee concept in Leviticus 25 – namely, that economic and social structures should provide the opportunity for economic restoration or redemption. Human capital is a key economic resource. It is perhaps the only modern equivalent to the land of the Old Testament and thus the principle that it can be restored or renewed is an important one. Employers need to have a firm commitment to training – the future for the unskilled in European labour markets is particularly bleak. It also means that there is a strong case for government intervention in the form of 'active labour-market policy': retraining and (if necessary compulsory) re-employment rather than indefinite payment of unemployment benefit. The emerging consensus on this amongst economists is encouraging.

However, the challenge of unemployment in Western Europe remains a very severe one, despite some recent improvements in most countries. The challenge, in policy terms, is to find appropriate methods of government intervention that correct market failures in labour markets, but do so in a way that does not undermine social cohesion. Perhaps this means that efforts need to be redoubled to encourage geographical mobility of capital rather than of labour. This means tailoring economic policies to the regional and community context, something that will be very difficult to achieve against an inherently deflationary, centralized European macroeconomic framework.

Satisfying the principle that everyone should have the opportunity to work is only half of the challenge. The other half is to make those employment opportunities rewarding and satisfying. Genesis 3: 17–19 instructs us that, after the Fall, we should not expect work to be easy – but easy work is not necessarily rewarding work and vice versa. There are no simple solutions here for this Christian agenda, but questioning the prevailing attitude of mind might be a good place to start. Thus economists might begin by modelling employment in a rather more imaginative way than as simply 'not leisure'.

Notes

[1] This paradigmatic nature of the nexus between God, his chosen people and the Promised Land and its economic implications is expounded in Christopher Wright, *Living as the People of God* (Leicester, 1983). As with any model, it attempts to distil and summarize. Nevertheless it provides a helpful basis for Christian ethical thinking about the economic order.

2 John Howard Yoder provides a fuller discussion of this suggestion in his *The Politics of Jesus*, 2nd edn (Grand Rapids, 1994).

3 Paul Marshall, 'Vocation, work and jobs', in Paul Marshall, Edward Vanderkloet, Peter Nijkamp, Sander Griffioen and Harry Antonides (eds.), *Labour of Love: Essays on Work* (Toronto, 1980), provides further discussion.

4 Quoted in David Landes, *The Wealth and Poverty of Nations* (London, 1998), 175.

5 Max Weber, 'Die protestantische Ethik und der "Geist" des Kapitalismus', *Archiv für Sozialwissenschaft und Sozialpolitik*, 20 (1904), 1–54; 21 (1905), 1–110.

6 Adam Smith did exalt 'ease', 'cleanliness' and 'honourableness' as desirable characteristics of employment. However, he thought that the non-pecuniary advantages of jobs with these characteristics would attract workers towards them in a free market, thus encouraging employers to provide such jobs through self-interest rather than for reasons of moral sentiment (Adam Smith, *The Wealth of Nations*, 1776).

7 Norman Hampson, *The Enlightenment* (Harmondsworth, 1968).

8 A non-exhaustive list includes the following: R. Blank, *Do Justice: Linking Christian Faith and Modern Economic Life* (Cleveland, OH, 1992); D. A. Hay, *Economics Today: A Christian Critique* (Leicester, 1989); John Paul II, *Laborem Exercens* (London, 1981); Oxford Declaration on Christian Faith and Economics, *Transformation*, 7/2 (1990), 1–9; J. P. Wogamon, *Economics and Ethics: A Christian Enquiry* (London, 1986).

9 Hay, *Economics Today*, 73–5.

10 William Temple, *Christianity and Social Order* (Harmondsworth, 1942; repr. London, 1976).

11 International evidence for this phenomenon is reported in E. Berman, J. Bound and S. Machin, 'Implications of skill-biased technological change: international evidence', *Quarterly Journal of Economics*, 113/4 (1998), 1245–79.

12 For example, Patrick Minford, *Unemployment, Cause and Cure*, 2nd edn (Oxford, 1985).

13 This tradition is evident in a long series of modern-era papal encyclicals commencing with Pius XI, *Rerum Novarum* (1891). This material is reprinted in D. J. O'Brien and T. A. Shannon, *Catholic Social Thought: The Documentary Heritage* (Maryknoll, NY, 1992).

14 Truman F. Bewley, 'A depressed labor market as explained by participants', *American Economic Review Papers and Proceedings*, 85 (1995), 250–4.

15 George Akerlof and Janet Yellen, *Efficiency Wage Models of Labour Markets* (Cambridge, 1986).

[16] Carl Shapiro and Joseph Stiglitz, 'Equilibrium unemployment as a worker discipline device', *American Economic Review*, 74 (June 1984), 433–44.

[17] George A. Akerlof, 'Gift exchange and efficiency-wage theory – 4 views', *American Economic Review*, 74/2 (1984), 79-83.

[18] Martin Weitzman, *The Share Economy: Conquering Stagflation* (Cambridge, 1986).

[19] Tony Atkinson and John Micklewright, 'Unemployment compensation and labour market transitions: a critical review', *Journal of Economic Literature*, 29 (December 1991), 1679–1727.

[20] Wiji Narendranathan and Mark Stewart, 'How does the benefit effect vary as unemployment spells lengthen?', *Journal of Applied Econometrics*, 8 (1993), 361–81.

[21] John Maynard Keynes, *The General Theory of Employment, Interest and Money* (London, 1936).

[22] Truman F. Bewley, 'A depressed labor market as explained by participants'.

[23] Ernst Fehr, Erich Kirchler, Andreas Weichbold and Simon Gächter, 'When social norms overpower competition: gift exchange in experimental labor markets', *Journal of Labor Economics*, 16/2 (1994), 324–51.

[24] Assar Lindbeck and Dennis Snower, *The Insider–Outsider Theory of Employment and Unemployment* (Cambridge, MA, 1989).

[25] The seminal paper on this is Olivier Blanchard and Lawrence Summers, 'Hysteresis and the European unemployment problem', *National Bureau of Economic Research Macroeconomics Annual* (Cambridge, MA, 1986), 16–78.

[26] See Andrew Henley and Euclid Tsakalotos, *Corporatism and Economic Performance* (Aldershot, 1993).

[27] Peter Elias and Mary Gregory, *The Changing Structure of Occupations and Earnings in Great Britain 1975–1990*, Department of Employment Research Series No. 27 (Sheffield, 1994), reported in Derek Bosworth, Peter Dawkins and Thorsten Stromback, *The Economics of the Labour Market* (London, 1996).

[28] See, for example, P. B. Doeringer and M. J. Piore, *Internal Labour Markets and Manpower Analysis* (Lexington, MA, 1971).

[29] Gary Becker, *The Economics of Discrimination* (Chicago, 1957).

[30] For the American context see Frank Levy, *Dollars and Dreams: The Changing American Income Distribution* (New York, 1988), and for the UK, Paul Gregg and Stephen Machin, 'Is the UK rise in inequality different?', in Ray Barrell (ed.), *The UK Labour Market* (Cambridge, 1994).

[31] Edward Lazear is one of the principal exponents of personnel

economics. His recent work is surveyed in his volume *Personnel Economics* (Cambridge, MA, 1996).

32 Dennis Snower, 'Evaluating unemployment policies: what do the underlying theories tell us?', *Oxford Review of Economic Policy*, 11/1 (1995), 110–35.

8

What is happening to the welfare state?

ANDREW DILNOT

For the last quarter of the twentieth century, in the UK and much of the rest of the developed world, the scale of the future welfare burden was at the heart of political and economic debate. After a century of largely tax-funded growth, through periods of enormous demographic, social and economic change, concerns about the possibility or consequences of further growth began to be voiced more and more frequently and across a wider political range. Perhaps because the welfare state is so emotive a subject, much of the debate has been rather vague, and on occasion confused and ill-informed. The provision of welfare is inevitably bound up with ethical judgements, so we should expect to be able to bring Christian faith to bear on this subject. My aim in this chapter is to set out the context for a coherent debate about what happens next.

In section 1, I discuss what it is we have in mind when we talk about the welfare state, and consider the way in which welfare activity has developed, explanations for the growth in spending, and how this has related to the development of overall state activity. Section 2 illustrates the impact of welfare spending on the distribution of income. Section 3 considers the policies of the current and immediately preceding governments, and draws out directions of change. In section 4, I attempt a description of some areas where Christians might want to pause before accepting the current prevailing terms of much of the debate in this field.

1. What is welfare and how did we get here?

'Welfare' and the 'welfare state' are not in general clearly defined, or understood to mean the same things in different countries. In the USA, for example, welfare is typically understood to cover what in the UK we would describe as means-tested benefits. For our purposes it seems best to think of welfare spending as being all spending on social security and personal social services, health and education, both in the public and private sectors.

Table 8.1 shows planned public spending in 1998–9 on the main items of the welfare state, in £bn, as an average amount per household in the UK, and as a share of national income. All these amounts are large – the welfare state absorbs most of public spending and therefore taxation, and accounts for around one-quarter of national income. In addition to this public spending, there are substantial amounts of 'private' welfare spending, such as that on private pensions, private health and private education services, which together account for around a further 7 per cent of national income.

The welfare state has been one of the most dramatic developments of the last 150 years, and particularly of the period since the Second World War. Figure 8.1 shows what has happened to public spending on the welfare state in real terms. The growth has been remarkable, and has led to an increase in the share of national income absorbed by these services from 12 to 30 per cent. This increase is at the heart of concerns about future increases in the 'burden' of welfare.

At least four broad sets of reasons seem to be significant in explaining the growth of welfare spending.

Growing affluence

It is easy to forget quite how rapidly real incomes have grown. Figure 8.2 shows the level of GDP in real terms over the twentieth century, reflecting an almost sevenfold increase. As individuals and nations grow more affluent, they tend to increase the share of

Table 8.1 Planned public spending in the UK, 1998–1999

	£bn	*% GDP*	*£000s per household*
Social security	95.5	11.8	3.8
Health	37.2	4.6	1.5
Education	38.2	4.7	1.5

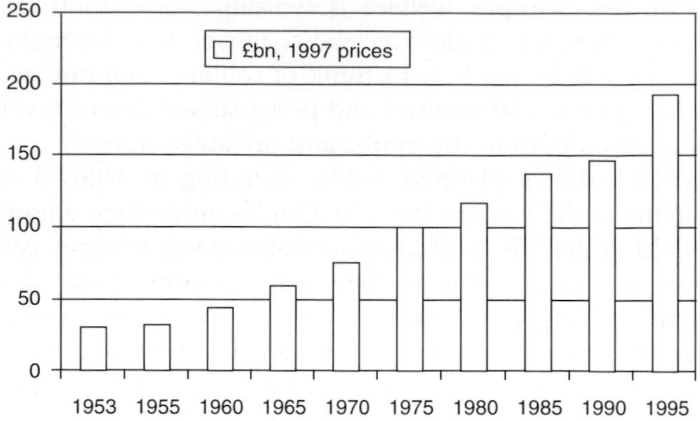

Figure 8.1 The growth of the welfare state

total spending devoted to some commodities and reduce the share devoted to others. Food is a clear example of something which tends to see a decline in budget share as income rises, while health, education and incomes in retirement, sickness and unemployment are all characterized by a tendency to increase their share as national income rises. It is easy to see why this is – at very low levels of income a small number of necessities such as food and shelter will dominate the budget, while as more resources become available, it becomes possible to shift towards activities which are in some sense less essential. As we continue to grow more affluent it seems likely that our desire to spend more on traditional welfare-state areas will persist, and at current trend rates of growth GDP, will double in real terms roughly every thirty years.[1]

Demographic change

This is an area that has been characterized by rather emotive public debate, but it is nonetheless true that a substantial part of welfare spending, broadly defined, is targeted on those over retirement age, and their numbers have grown significantly in the post-war period, and will do so again in the twenty-first century.[2] Since almost half of the social security budget goes to this group, and health spending is also weighted heavily to the last years of life, this has tended to increase actual and desired spending. This

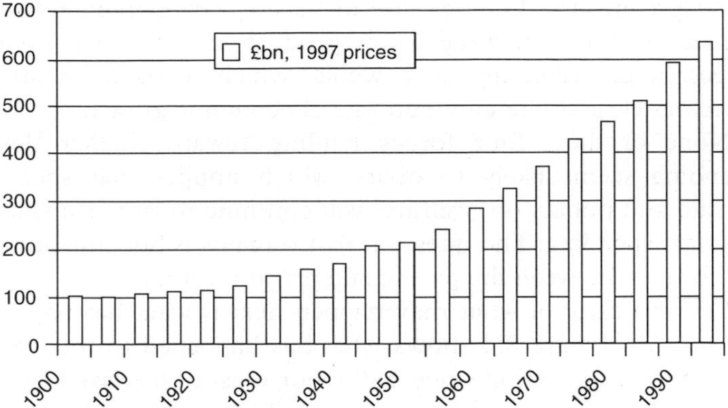

Figure 8.2 National income, 1900–1995

is, of course, in one way a reflection of increased affluence, which has facilitated the increased longevity which partly explains these changes.

Technology

Advances in technology can have two very different effects on the cost of delivering goods and services. Advances which make existing activities easier, cheaper or more effective should save money, and there are many examples of technological change which have had this effect, notably in the health service. But technological change also delivers new possibilities which may themselves be expensive, albeit of great value. New drugs can offer genuine benefit, but also substantial cost. Less dramatically perhaps, new computing technology can offer exciting educational opportunities, but can be expensive to acquire, and may require retraining for teaching staff. The onward march of technology seems unlikely to slow.

Labour intensity/wages

Social security, the largest welfare activity in both public and private sectors, is largely a transfer of money from one group of people to another, or from one time in an individual's life to another. Health and education, by contrast, are highly labour-intensive services. In both these areas, not least because of the development of technology and increasing expectations reflecting increased affluence, wage levels need at least to keep up with wages in the economy as a whole, which tends to mean real increases close to the long-run rate of economic growth.

None of these four forces tending towards higher desired spending seems likely to abate, which implies that spending, private and public, on 'welfare' will continue to rise as a share of national spending. The question that remains is how this increase will be split between the public and private sectors.

One indicator of what may happen next is what has happened in the past. Figure 8.3 shows what has happened to total public spending in the period since 1890. For most of the last 100 years there has been an upward trend in public spending. Substantial rises occurred during each of the world wars, with the decline at the end of each war leaving spending much higher than its pre-war level. Spending rose from around 10 per cent of national income in 1890 to reach almost 50 per cent by the early 1970s. This growth in public spending was funded by a corresponding growth in taxation as increasing affluence allowed simultaneous increases in personal disposable income and in the burden of taxation. Much of the growth to the mid-1970s reflected the development of welfare-state spending. But in the mid-1970s the growth stopped.

The immediate cause was the so-called IMF crisis: the economy had stagnated, inflation was high and public-sector borrowing reached almost 10 per cent of national income. The then Labour

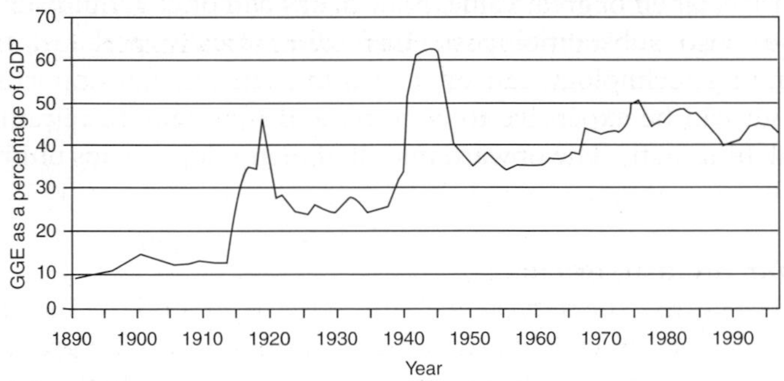

Figure 8.3 Government expenditure as a proportion of GDP, 1890 to present day

government agreed to cut public spending. The mood against both taxing and spending seemed rapidly to set firm. Cutting taxes and slimming down the state became the almost uniform objective for successful politicians, and, even though substantial reductions were rarely achieved, the growth was stopped, in the UK at least.

Many explanations have been offered for the swing against government spending. At one level, the sense of the ability of governments to achieve, so strong during and after the Second World War, was much damaged by the mid-1970s. And the sense that government could do harm, both through taxation and public spending, became more firmly established. There is no doubt that policies such as 98 per cent top income tax rates were difficult to make sense of, and even some parts of the social security system could cause problems. But too often these problems – which were typically marginal to the overall activity of government, and cheaply changed, affecting relatively few people – were felt to be symptomatic of a problem affecting all tax and public spending. So we moved, for example, from the clearly reasonable statement that a 98 per cent top income tax rate is seriously damaging to incentives, to the idea that cutting the basic rate of income tax from 25 to 23 per cent might have a large impact on behaviour, or the current notion that a 20 per cent starting rate of income tax might damage incentives and so we should move to a 10 per cent rate. This is an area where much caution is needed. And on the general question of whether taxes are in some sense 'too high', we should remember two things. First, taxes are used to buy something: they are not simply thrown away. Second, as shown by Table 8.2, we are by European standards a very low tax country overall, and it continues to be difficult to prove a link between overall tax burdens and economic performance.[3]

Levels of public spending as share of national income still fluctuate with the economic cycle in the UK, but there is little sign of a return to sustained growth in the public sector. Despite the decline in overall public spending, we have seen a continued increase in public spending on welfare items as a share of national income, which has been achieved by cutting the share of other forms of public spending. Capital spending was one of the early victims of the post-IMF crisis spending cuts, and governments have repeatedly found it easier to cut planned capital spending than spending on recurrent items. The reduction in defence

Table 8.2 Tax as a share of national income in OECD countries

Country	*% of income*	*Country*	*% of income*
UK	38	Spain	40
USA	32	Portugal	43
France	51	Greece	38
Germany	45	Canada	44
Netherlands	48	Japan	32
Sweden	61	Belgium	50
Denmark	55	Australia	35
Italy	48	New Zealand	48

spending as a share of GDP has been as dramatic in the last fifteen years, but much less noticed. As a consequence of these and other changes, the share of total public spending going to welfare-state spending has grown dramatically, as shown in Figure 8.4.

The outcome of these changes is that there is little left to cut in the non-welfare-state public sector. The current New Labour government is committed to a small increase in public-sector capital spending, albeit only to the levels of the mid-1990s. And the welfare state itself has not escaped. During the period between the Second World War and 1980, social security benefit levels in the UK broadly kept pace with growing living standards, which saw a more than doubling of their real level. Since 1980, most

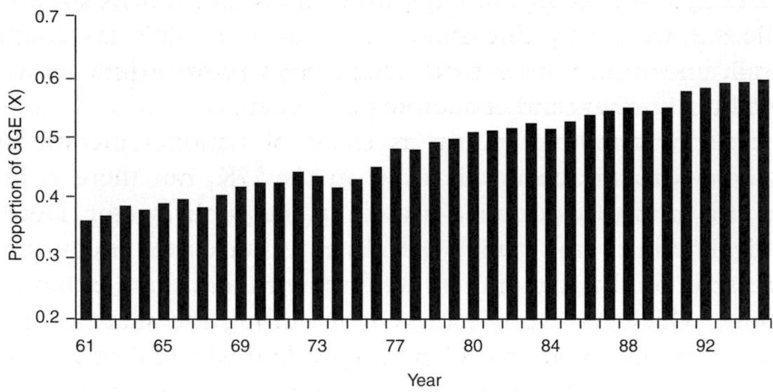

Figure 8.4 Composition of public spending: proportion of spending on education, health and social security

benefit levels have been held constant in real terms, and there has been a steady shift towards greater reliance on means-tested benefits. Cuts in widows' benefits, the means-testing of incapacity benefit and a decision to continue with only price indexation of the flat-rate state pension are all indications that the New Labour government is set to continue down much the same route as its Conservative predecessor, although it is striking that the new government has increased means-tested benefit levels such as the working families' tax credit, and has set an aim of increasing the means-tested benefit for the retired in line with earnings.

One consequence of these policies has been that, unlike many of our neighbours, the UK does not face a crisis in the financing of state pensions.[4] The National Insurance contribution rate needed to fund the pension will fall between now and the middle of the twenty-first century, despite the very large increase in the number receiving a pension, for the simple reason that the pension will fall from around 15 per cent of average earnings to around 8 per cent. The crisis the state pension faces in the UK is not one of tax rises, but of declining value relative to the living standards of the population as a whole.

These changes in state social security have both driven and been enabled by the growth of private provision. If state pensions fail to increase to reflect growing affluence, then those who can afford to will make provision of their own. Indeed, in its recent Green Paper[5] the government was quite explicit that its objective in this field was that, while total spending on pensions should grow, the share of that spending done by the state should fall.

While it is clearly in social security that the private finance and provision of welfare-type activities has developed furthest, it is by no means only here that these trends are seen.[6] Private spending on both education and health more than trebled in real terms between 1979–80 and 1995–96, to £6.4 billion and £8.7 billion respectively. These increases were from 8 per cent of all education spending to 18 per cent, and from 11 per cent of all health spending to 18 per cent.[7] Although this growth has been rapid, the level of private spending on health and education is not high by international standards, in contrast to the picture for pensions. Nothing that has happened since the mid-1990s leads to any expectations that these trends would change.

2. The impact of public provision

In this section I look at the impact of this public-sector activity. Figure 8.5 shows the level of income before government intervention – 'original' income – and after – 'final income' – at each point in the income distribution, starting with the 20 per cent of the population with the lowest income, quintile 1, and going through to the richest 20 per cent, quintile 5. Figure 8.6 subtracts tax payments from public spending to show the net impact of government activity.[8]

The effect of government activity is highly redistributive; indeed, it is hard to make sense of the activities of government in any other framework. A very large proportion of all taxes is paid by a minority of high-income households – the top 1 per cent of income taxpayers pay 20 per cent of all the income tax paid, the top 10 per cent pay 50 per cent. While other taxes are less progressive, Figure 8.5 shows that the share of all taxes paid at the top is still high. The benefits of spending are more evenly spread and, in the case of social security, focused on the lower part of the income distribution. This is in many ways unsurprising, but it is a reminder that in purely financially self-interested terms the effect of government is to leave those who pay for most of the activity significantly worse off. That is not to say either that it is wrong, or that the better off oppose this activity, simply that an attempt to explain it using a parody of economics that suggests that financial self-interest is the only or dominant motivation is doomed to fail.

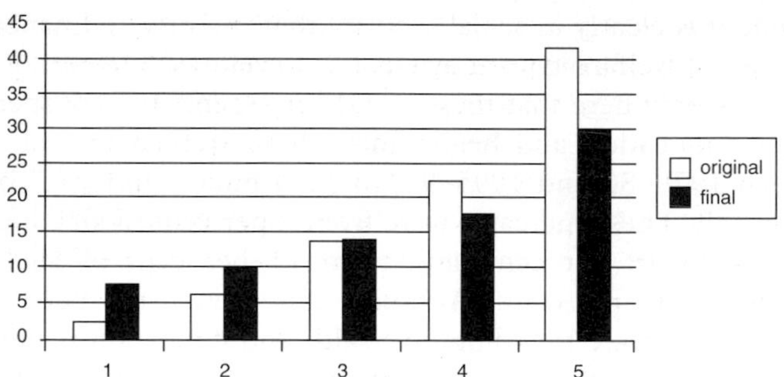

Figure 8.5 Incomes before and after government intervention

Source: 'The impact of taxes and benefits on household income 1996–1997', *Economic Trends*, 533 (April 1998).

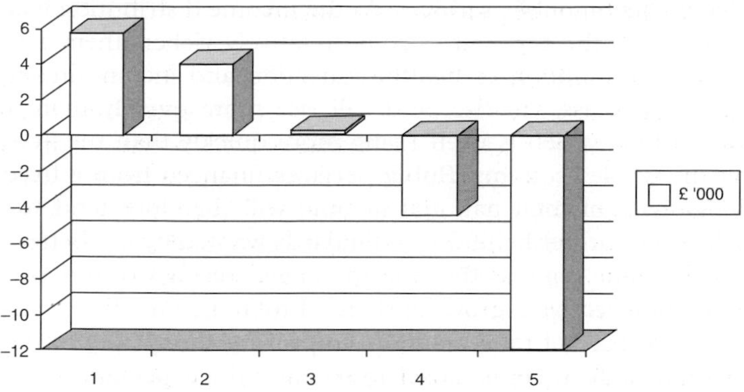

Figure 8.6 Net impact of government activity

Source: 'The impact of taxes and benefits on household income 1996–1997', *Economic Trends*, 533 (April 1998).

The principal explanation for the extent of the redistribution is simply that it is the deliberate intent of policy. We choose to have a tax-funded health-care system delivering universal care free at the point of use. And in social security we now choose to be even more redistributive by moving away from universal benefits funded by taxation towards means-tested benefits funded by taxation. But there is a second explanation, which is the large and growing level of underlying inequality. The top 1 per cent of income taxpayers pay so large a share of income tax not principally because the tax system is especially progressive, but because their incomes are so high relative to those of the rest of the population. In 1996–7 the top 1 per cent of income-tax payers had annual incomes in excess of £76,100, while the top 10 per cent had incomes in excess of £28,300.

It has become almost a commonplace observation that the distribution of income has widened in recent decades. In part this has reflected price indexation of social security benefits, in part the growth of lone parenthood and of unemployment, but most important of all, a widening in the underlying distribution of earnings.[8] Having stabilized in the first half of the 1990s, there is now evidence that inequality in incomes is rising again.[9] The widening of the income distribution is a serious problem for government, not simply for its direct consequences, but because of its impact on public services. As the income distribution widens and those in the top half become relatively richer, their desired level of consumption of health, education and income in retirement or sickness will rise, and will rise more quickly than their total income, which is itself rising more quickly than the average over the whole economy. Public services financed from a fixed or falling share of total national income will therefore tend to fall further and further behind the standards wanted by the better off.

At the same time, as those in the higher reaches of the income distribution receive a growing share of total income, they will pay a growing share of total taxation. Improving the quality of public provision so as to come closer to meeting the expectations of the better off means either cutting some other area of public spending, or raising taxes. But any tax increase will bear heavily on those on higher incomes, who will not typically receive anything like the same share of any increase in public spending. There is a genuine difficulty for governments.

3. Where are we going now?

The central tension faced by governments is between the widespread desire to spend more on welfare-type activities, and the belief of politicians, apparently vindicated by voting patterns, that tax increases are unacceptable.[10] Alongside this is a widely shared objective of, at least, protecting the most vulnerable. One response to the problem facing governments is to cut non-welfare programmes so as to increase spending on welfare. This was a path well trodden by the 1974–9 Labour government and the 1979–97 Conservative government. While it has obvious attractions to whoever is in power, there is little further scope.

A second response is to increase taxes in relatively invisible ways, and use this money to pay for a growing share of public spending. This is another route much loved of all governing parties, but has not enabled a significant increase in the overall tax level in recent decades, and seems unlikely to. A third response is to accept that public provision can no longer be increased, and that further increases in the share of national spending devoted to a particular area must come through increases in private spending. This response has effectively now been made by all of the major political parties with respect to the provision of pensions, which is the single largest item of both public and private welfare spending.

This third response is a central part of the New Labour government's policies. We have seen since 1997 substantial increases in the generosity of a number of benefits, but they have typically been means-tested: the working families' tax credit, the minimum income guarantee, increases in the child amounts in income support. For a government committed to increasing generosity to those on low incomes within an overall constraint on the level of spending and taxation, such a route is natural, although the contrast with the commitment to universal benefits seen in earlier Labour Party governments is striking.

A fourth response is to try to reduce the number of people who need to rely on social security by emphasizing self-reliance and encouraging people into paid work. The working families' tax credit is designed to 'make work pay', while the New Deal is a series of programmes seeking to help people back into the labour market. The New Labour government has described its strategy in this area as 'work for those who can, support for those who can't'.

4. Concerns

The welfare state attracts strong feelings and is the subject of widespread disagreements. This section briefly describes four areas where Christians might be concerned to challenge implicit or explicit judgements often made in the debate about welfare policy.

Valuing people

Work is important, self-reliance can be laudable: it is not difficult for Christians to agree to such statements and applaud government policies which make it easier for individuals to do paid work and to become financially self-reliant. Policies like the New Deal or encouragement for private pension provision can be welcomed. But it is easy to move from encouraging these potentially good things to believing that they are prerequisites to full 'membership' of society. In particular, there is a risk that we begin to value people by their 'contributions' to society or the economy, rather than by their value in God's sight. This seems clearly wrong.

Asserting ownership

Almost all discussion of the economy and certainly of the welfare state assumes and accepts a particular view of property rights – that we 'own' our salaries, our houses, our pension rights. It is widely accepted that governments may impose taxes, but this is generally seen as something that requires the consent of the population. The distribution of incomes is a reflection of these accepted property rights. But these property rights have little or no basis in Christian understanding of the world. We are stewards, not owners, and are reminded that all things come from God, and are ultimately his. We must not fall into the trap of feeling that our material good (or ill) fortunes are a reflection of some final and right or merited distribution of property rights.

Redistribution and financial self-interest

A related concern is about redistribution and self-interest. There is common acceptance of the idea that financial self-interest is the major driving force of modern economics and life, and that to behave in a way inconsistent with it is foolish and impractical. This is simply wrong. It is true that, faced with two identical loaves of bread, one of which is twice as expensive as the other, I am likely to buy the cheaper loaf. But this does not mean that it would be irrational for me to give the loaf I buy to someone who is hungry, or to buy the expensive loaf because the baker was in need, or simply to give the money I might have spent on the loaf to someone else who seemed to need it. All these sorts of things happen, and much the most dramatic way in which they happen is through the payment of taxes which are then spent on highly redistributive services like social security, health or education. We must not slide from thinking that, in general, it makes sense when faced with identical commodities to choose that with the lower price, to thinking that in all our behaviour we are to be entirely self-interested. We are not, and should not be.

Incentives

Much of the debate about the welfare state focuses on the problems of the distorting impact of state provision on behaviour. The classic example is individuals choosing not to do paid work, but instead to rely on receipt of social security benefits. Such behaviour will exist, but we should also recognize that many will do what is right, not least because work is itself a good thing which has a value to the worker beyond the money she or he is paid. We should be at least as unwilling to believe that all will behave badly as we are to believe that all will behave well.

Conclusion

Spending on welfare-state-type activities is substantial across the developed world. We can make little sense of this activity in a model of purely self-interested behaviour – welfare states were introduced and persist to achieve explicitly ethically motivated outcomes. For Christians, there is work to do in establishing which outcomes should be sought, and in standing out for the value of every individual; the truths that we are stewards, not owners; that we are not and should not be always self-interested; and that individuals will sometimes do what is right.

Notes

1 See C. Emmerson and A. Dilnot, 'The economic environment', in X. Halsey (ed.), *British Social Trends in the Twentieth Century* (forthcoming).

2 See R. Disney, *Can We Afford to Grow Older? A Perspective on the Economics of Aging* (Cambridge, MA, 1996) for a careful analysis.

3 Since the South East Asian financial crisis, we have heard fewer assertions that the low tax burdens there are linked to those countries' economic performance.

4 See P. Johnson, *Older Getting Wiser* (London, 1999).

5 DSS, *A New Contract for Welfare: Partnership in Pensions* (London, 1998).

6 See T. Burchardt, J. Hills and C. Propper, *Private Welfare and Public Policy* (York, 1999).

7 Ibid.

8 On the distribution of income generally, see A. Goodman, P. Johnson and S. Webb, *Inequality in the UK* (Oxford, 1997); on the distribution of earnings, see A. Gosling, S. Machin and C. Meghir, 'What has happened to the wages of men since 1966?', in J. Hills (ed.), *New Inequalities: The Changing Distribution of Income and Wealth in the United Kingdom* (Cambridge, 1996).

9 DSS, *Households below Average Income* (London, 1998).

10 See R. Jowell, J. Curtice, A. Park, L. Brook and K. Thomson (eds.),

British Social Attitudes: The Thirteenth Report (Aldershot, 1998) for a detailed analysis.

[11] T. Besley, J. Hall and I. Preston, 'Private health insurance and the state of the NHS', *Commentary*, 52 (London, 1996).

9

Economic growth: is more always better?

BOB GOUDZWAARD

Have you ever noticed how many jokes are made about economists? They seem to share with theologians the burden of awkward hilarity. But whereas jokes about theologians are often good-natured – a theologian is someone who throws dust in the air and then complains that he can no longer see clearly! – the humour about economists is more pointed. Some remarks, such as the comment that economists would rather use each other's toothbrush than each other's terminology, are still good-natured. But other comments – 'economics is common sense made difficult', or economics is a 'dismal science' (Carlyle) – are more biting. And what should we think about the following story? Mrs Margaret Thatcher, on a visit to Moscow, was observing a military parade. After a succession of massive nuclear missiles had trundled past, there followed a group of shuffling, dishevelled, gloomy-looking men in raincoats and sloppy hats. When she expressed astonishment at these, the Soviet leaders explained: 'these are our economists, for they have the greatest destructive potential!'

However that may be, it is of course not my intention here to concentrate on the strange habits, the dismal traditions and possibly the destructive potential of economists. That could be diverting, but only briefly. My focus, rather, grows out of a mixed sense of concern and curiosity: a concern about the obviously growing dominance of the culture of economics in our society; and a curiosity about the role which modern economists play in the background. For jokes, such as the ones I have just mentioned, betray the uneasiness which many people feel about the economists' doings as members of a strange and alien sub-culture. Many people have obviously become aware that a growing number of problems in our time are economic in nature, and further, that these are seldom solved: such as the problem of worldwide poverty, but also the existence of poverty in the midst of even very wealthy societies; problems such as stress in the workplace and of lasting unemployment; and the problem of a continous environmental degradation. And so the doubt grows: is the way in which economists and politicians deal with our problems really trustworthy? Or, somewhat deeper: are the assumptions which underlie the present culture of economics realistic? Behind these doubts one feels a creeping suspicion that the standard way that economists think is itself one of the main causes of the growing domination of the economy and of economic yardsticks in our culture.

It is not, of course, that all economists agree. Even economists who are Christians have their differences, just as they have different toothbrushes. But at least one thing they will have in common: the conviction, related to their Christian faith, that no assumption, and no standard of the culture of economics, can from the outset be elevated beyond critique. For it is contrary to faith itself to cherish the escape-route of the neutrality or self-sufficiency of science. The Christian faith teaches us that world-views do matter, even in economic logic and reasoning, and these world-views of course include the critical biblical view of humanity, nature and society.

I do not say this, however, to defend a kind of ideological a priori. It is not my intention, to be sure, to develop a specific branch of 'Christian economics', which we could for example place next to an Islamic or a general humanistic type of economics. No, I do not propose to withdraw behind the walls of a Christian fortress. On the contrary, I propose the opposite: namely, that Christian economists should broaden and deepen the *general* view or perspective which 'standard' economics holds on humans, nature and society. Further, I contend that they should do this especially at this time, at the turn of the millennium, when a large number of unsolved economic problems have emerged. For I suspect that there is a relationship between, on the one hand, the superficiality of the dominant assumptions of the present culture of economics and, on the other hand, the often inadequate reaction of economists to the problems of our time.

This point is so important that a practical illustration from my own experience may be useful. Some years ago I was asked as a European economist to serve on an interdisciplinary research group on the welfare crisis in the United States. Our central question was: why had poverty in the USA become so persistent? Further, why was it growing year on year, almost regardless of whether Democrats or Republicans were in the White House? To our surprise, our research group, which included some people from the US urban ghettoes, found that at least a part of the explanation was related to the narrowness of the paradigms of modern social scientists. And especially of those scientists – the economists, the political scientists, the sociologists – who served as expert advisers to the government and the various political parties. The influence which academicians have on the political debate in the USA is so widespread that there is a special word for it: academocracy. And we found that the persistence of poverty could be traced to the influence of academocracy. For example, there is an ongoing debate in the USA between Democrats and Republicans on 'welfare' versus 'workfare'. One side, the Keynesian welfare approach, accentuates the need for more spending on the poor; the other side, the neo-classical workfare approach, stresses the need for stronger incentives to get people to accept work and to go to work. We asked ourselves, why only these two approaches? Both are strongly symptom-related and, furthermore, they both deal with poor people more as objects than as social or economic subjects. The answer was in fact simple: this is the standard way that economic textbooks treat poverty. The textbooks pay scant attention to causes of growing poverty like social exclusion[1] and economic enrichment, or to the possible role of the poor themselves. So political measures such as the fiscal demotivation of enrichment and the strengthening of community development by the poor are easily neglected, whereas they could be at the very heart of the problem.[2] Hidden world-views can thus disorientate not only academic disciplines, but also the state and structure of society.

Now if this is true, it has wider implications. It leads for instance to an interesting question: do economists approach the issue of *economic growth* from an equally narrow academic perspective which has affected the formation of the general cultural and political opinion? That question will be my main concern in this chapter, and it seems very important to me. For no claims in our modern society are more insistent and compelling than those related to the necessity of continued economic growth. Growth is seen as the basis of almost everything which is good and desirable. It is the basis of more jobs and of the reduction of the public deficit; it is the basis of the maintenance of a good health and social security system; it is the basis of more adequate environmental protection and increased development aid. So it is our culture's common conviction that we have to strive for the highest degree of productivity and competitiveness in our economy – even if this at times requires substantial sacrifices in human relationships and natural resources. This way of thinking, I believe, is one of the roots of the growing dominance of economics in our culture, for in it we allow economic yardsticks to be decisive in most cases. But is this standard way of reasoning correct? Further, is it the only possible way of thinking? Do its underlying theoretical assumptions need critical testing – for instance, from the broader perspective which the Bible provides?

Questions like these have puzzled me for many years. Almost thirty years ago, in my thesis about unpriced scarcity, I began wrestling with them academically.[3] I have also dealt with them politically, as for example in 1976 when I wrote the central parts of the programme 'Not by Bread Alone', the election platform of the Christian political parties in the Netherlands. But these questions have never been as urgent as they are now. We are living in a time of intense globalization in which all modern nations feel compelled to maintain and expand their so-called competitive advantage over other nations. Competitiveness and growth have now become the new absolutes for all so-called good government. We have to expand economically simply to exist: 'I am growing, therefore I am'. And all this is happening at a time when serious warnings can be heard: that this competitive struggle between the rich countries is diminishing the chances for the poorest countries; also that a continuous expansion of production and trade is threatening the diminishing carrying capacity of the earth and is destabilizing the world's climates.[4] But, we hear, do we have any choice? Is there any viable alternative at the turn of this millennium? In this spirit both Shell and the World Trade Organization took over Mrs Thatcher's well-known TINA slogan:

'There Is No Alternative'. Their implicit message is that so-called doomsday-thinkers should keep their mouths shut.

At this point the discussion can easily turn grim – as is usually the case when implicit assumptions come to the fore. I am always happy to engage in abstract debate with fellow economists, but in this chapter I propose to widen the discourse by discussing briefly the biblical sources of my own academic inspiration. For it could very well be that exactly those sources are needed to overcome impasses like the ones to which I have been referring, and lead to a fresh reappraisal of some of the most compelling issues of our time.

Let me begin by referring to a spiritual impulse which comes directly from many passages in the New Testament. In his parables Jesus often spoke about stewards, good stewards and bad stewards (for example, Matthew 20: 8; Luke 12: 42). And behind his words you feel a deep respect for the God-given rule of *oikonomia*, the good care which is needed for the *oikos*, the household. For Jesus, the word economy – Gk *oikonomia* – was primarily a divine mandate. It included the care of the land and a concern for the well-being of those who live from its fruits. So for Jesus, it was an economic and not just an ethical rule that workers should receive their food on time! Remarkably in Jesus' words about human economic life there is also an eschatological perspective. The Lord of the land himself will come back to ask all his servants to render account of their style of economic behaviour (Luke 16: 1ff.). And that accountability is not only required of persons but also of the *ethnē*, the peoples or nations of this world (Matthew 25: 32). It is not least as the Great Economist that God will judge them all.[5]

Now at first glance these references may seem unrelated to the present debate about economic growth. But let us not be too quick to jump to that conclusion. In these New Testament texts, economy, responsibility and accountability are closely interrelated; they simply cannot be separated. But, we may ask, how far have we succeeded in separating them, for instance by splitting them into two compartments – physical and metaphysical? This is an intriguing question, for we can ask this equally about scientific economics and about our societies as a whole. On the level of our modern society the question runs like this: have we built our society on the silent premiss that we can avoid a lot of nasty questions about responsibility and economic accountability – including questions of growth – if we simply turn to the factual world which functions by mechanisms which are in principle infallible? And on the level of economics as a science the question runs: have we as economists, precisely because we wanted to be as neutral and as scientifically objective as possible, fallen into a world-view that is too mechanical, that is closed to any kind of value-oriented normativity? One of the main characteristics of our subculture as economists is this: we want above all to be seen and valued as competent scientists. We have wanted this recognition at least since John Stuart Mill, who protested against Auguste Comte's refusal to view economics as a legitimate positive science.[6]

I believe it is important to ask these critical questions – not least in evaluating economic growth. For if we economists strive for value-freedom at all costs, then in the first place we will be unwilling to speak even one critical word about the quantity and quality of what human beings want. We will treat all these desires simply as data, as given factors; so our study of economic growth will concentrate on questions of the use and allocation of means, and will avoid the question of the choice of ends. In the second place, because we want to avoid all qualitative and subjective opinions, we will also speak only about objectively measurable entitities, like quantities and prices. And thereby our approach as economists to the issue of economic growth becomes shrunken and small. Our main concern is with attaining a maximum expansion of an output which is well allocated; that is, an output in which the allocation of all products is guided by a properly functioning market mechanism.

Do you not agree that in this way a reduction has taken place? This way of thinking regards economic resources like labour and land instrumentally; they become objects of use, not objects of care. This way of thinking, therefore, leads to a lack of an economic critique on the commercially promoted explosion of human needs in our already rich societies. For needs can be produced just as commodities are produced, notably by the input of the seductive devices which are offered by mass media. So the final result can be that, instead of a decrease of scarcity, an increase of scarcity is taking place. Think here for instance of e-commerce and advertising campaigns which push the level of human needs and desires artificially beyond the level of their possible saturation.

And all this is confirmed by what we daily see around us. We live in a post-modern society in which there is both an abundance of information and a growing general sense of scarcity, for which increasingly more growth is needed. Our society is also characterized by a reduced sense of economic accountability and care: for the market mechanism is not the best possible compass to guide us to a good outcome.

However, critique alone does not help. We should therefore not evade the question of alternatives. In a time in which the need for a stronger economic growth has become so strongly compelling, is it true that 'there is no alternative'? Here I want to draw your attention to a second source of inspiration: the biblical texts relating to the economic life of ancient Israel. I read these texts anew when I, as a young university lecturer, was asked to teach a course in the theory of economic systems. To my surprise I found that the regulations of the Torah about work and interest, land and rest, were the ingredients of a complete and coherent economic system.[7] Then this thought occurred to me: in this system of Torah economics, is there perhaps a hidden wisdom which might have value for our time?

Now it may seem absurd even to ask this question. For referring to the Torah means dealing with the rules and institutions of a totally different society, which was primarily agricultural in nature. And these rules and institutions are old – four millennia old. But this sense of remoteness may begin to change if we note that every economic system, of whatever historical period, has to find a kind of internal balance between necessary inputs and desirable outputs. In ancient Israel this balance was in some sense unique, or in any case was remarkably different from all modern market – and planned – economies. Let me try to explain. When we economists refer to the increase of the GDP (Gross Domestic Product) or GNP (Gross National Product) as an index of our economic growth, we know that these indexes represent outputs – the sum of all the values which were added to the economy by the overall expansion of the output-level. But to enable such an increase in *output*, a corresponding rise of *input* is needed in terms of the use of labour, capital and natural resources. Of course, economic systems can differ markedly in their adherence to either market or planning principles, but they can also differ in their primary orientation to either the level of output or input. In all modern economies the primary orientation is to the level of output. We want to maximize the growth of our production, and we therefore implement and enforce stringent rules of efficiency and productivity in the area of input. But in ancient Israel the primary economic orientation was to inputs. Just look what this meant in Israel with regard to the main production factors of labour, nature and capital. Labour: in Israel it was not allowed to subject any labourer to harsh treatment – a slave was immediately freed if only one tooth was knocked out, and all workers were entitled to enjoy their daily and weekly rest. Further, the land, the vital economic factor in ancient Israel, was protected by numerous legal measures. Every seventh year – the sabbatical year – the land was to be rested from cultivation, while it was fertilized by the cattle, so it would be ready for a new cycle of cultivation. And capital? It was made available for all people. This was arranged by an open and public discouragement of any strong accumulation of capital. For example, investment in land was impossible in Israel, because the Jubilee laws required it every forty-nine years to be returned to its original owners. So the demand for capital and the supply of capital could indeed meet each other around a zero-level of interest. All this made Israel a mainly input-orientated economy: the good and healthy condition of land, labour, capital and environment was basic to all economic processes and was enabled by an overall preventive care – a care which included even access to the land for the poor.

Of course such a radical orientation of an economy towards the preservation and regeneration of inputs has a price: it diminishes the possible final level of output. But in ancient Israel the height of that level was of secondary importance. For the soil was fertile enough to lead to good harvests, the needs of the people were limited, and extraordinary outputs were seen as surpluses which enabled feasting together, enjoying the abundance of the Lord with all the members of the community. For all the Israelites knew, and maybe they knew it better than we do, there can only be a sense of abundance if there is first an awareness of having enough – for, literally, abundance means *overflowing*, having even more than enough.

Let us consider this in light of our contemporary values. At first sight this looks plain crazy: this attentiveness to the condition of inputs and the apparent recklessness on the output side. But is that really true? To put it pointedly: why, when we speak of economic growth, do we only talk about the *volume* of the output side of our economies and never about the *condition* of the input side? Have we, in our Western economies, become so preoccupied with outer growth that we have neglected the possibility of an inner growth of our economies?

I think that the answer is an unequivocal 'yes'. In our rich societies we are now even reaching the point – indeed, there are indications that we have already passed it[8] – where the value of further increases of the outer growth is more than offset by reductions in the inner growth of the economy. Just think of the many people in the production process who are working under permanent stress and are facing 'burn-out'; in the Netherlands this amounts to one-sixth of the working population. Think also of the millions of people who have become unemployed for similar reasons. And think about the ease with which we accept further burdens on our environment, greater destruction of the fertile topsoil and the build-up of greenhouse gases, merely to reach a somewhat higher level of outer growth. And think last but not least about the lack of available and cheap capital, especially for poor people and for the indebted countries – precisely because we, as rich countries, want to give priority to our own consumption and output. In our economies the balance between inner and outer growth has become distorted; it has shifted far too much to the output side. Somehow in our modern arrogance we have missed the wisdom of ancient Israel, whose economy was an economy of abundance (*shalom*) and inclusion on the basis of limited means. In contrast, ours is an economy of scarcity and exclusion on the basis of an ever-expanding flow of means.

Now this insight could be a key for the liberation of our economies for which so many in our societies are looking. But how can we use that key? We obviously have to redress a balance. But how can we, in our countries and cultures, imagine an alternative? I would like to make two suggestions.

My first suggestion is derived from the wisdom which is evident in every growing tree. The tree grows in height, which relates to outer economic growth; but it grows also inwardly, in the silent process of building up its fruit-bearing capacity. This happens by the inclusion of all cells and by an enriching symbiosis with its environment. This combination of inner and outer growth is something that we have not been able to realize in our 'tunnel-economies'. For we include some people but exclude others – those who stay unemployed or are living in the poor South – and we increasingly overburden our natural environment and cause stress in a lot of human bodies and souls by the way in which we are producing things. And so the question occurs: how can a simple tree do what we are unable to do, combining those various goals and keeping the balance? The answer is as simple as it is surprising. The tree is able to do this by using restraints, by refraining from the desire to grow up to the heavens and to reach the clouds. At a certain moment, led by what we could call an in-built wisdom, the tree reaches maturity; it stops its further vertical growth in order to use its reserves fully to bear fruits and produce seeds.

In my view this analogy contains a valuable lesson for all modern economists and politicians. Only when we exercise restraint, only when we invoke the discipline of withholding, does inner economic growth become a real possibility.[9] The wisdom of self-limitation can be partially illustrated by the success of the Dutch *polder* model. This is a model of co-operation between the organizations of employers and employees, which make contracts with each other about the creation of more workplaces of a human-friendly and environmentally friendly type and which agree to uphold essential welfare provisions in the Netherlands, all of this on the basis of openness to restraint in the area of their financial claims. Notably, the labour unions have been willing to support a trade-off between these broader goals and the maximum rise in their own disposible wage-income. Of course, these contracts are sometimes difficult to make; the negotiations can be hard. But experience has shown that it works, even in a highly export-oriented economy like Holland which will lose out completely if it fails to maintain its high level of competitiveness.

My second suggestion is related to the almost forgotten need for an enlarged, broadened type of economic responsibility. For too long our societies have trusted well-functioning mechanisms, like the market mechanism, the democratic mechanism and even the plan mechanism, to produce good outcomes. Mechanisms, however, cannot save us. They can even tempt us to neglect basic responsibilities for our neighbours, for our environment, for the well-being of our children and grandchildren. So while we think that we are wide awake and alert, we can in fact be asleep, hypnotized by the soft and seductive voices that lull us into thinking that we should not fear, because Growth is with us and the staff of the Market will help us and lead us through all valleys of economic death.

But I am convinced that the time has come to wake up. Think of the parable of Jesus (Matthew 25: 1ff.), in which those who were fast asleep were awakened with the shout that the Lord was coming. Our situation is analogous. For our environment is in genuine peril, nations in the South are really perishing, and we are overburdening both others and ourselves. So the moment has come for our rich economies to leave childishness behind and to come of age; it is time for us to decide deliberately for enoughness, for contentment, wherever (and whenever) that is needed for the transformation of our economies. For if such a willingness were to grow in our culture, it could induce at least some, and maybe in the course of time a growing number of, producing companies to extend their economic services to the public, producing their goods with better care for the environment, less stressful labour conditions and a fairer compensation for their trading partners in the South, in exchange for either higher prices or lower wage demands. Labour unions could then consider whether they would be willing to pay for this in terms of a diminution of their wage claims, while consumers would have the choice to opt for a socially and ecologically 'better' product in exchange for a somewhat higher price. For 'always more' is the silliest formula to live by, and our task as Christians is primarily one of support and restraint.

Likewise, governments, according to a suggestion of George Goyder, could play a part in this. They could designate companies which are pioneers in the field of enlarged and widened forms of social and environmental responsibility with the label 'public company', so that these would be clearly recognizable by the public.[10] We should also expect our governments to take action in the international field. Our governments should not only be willing to co-operate in and conclude global agreements about environmental restraints (Rio, Kyoto), they should also be prepared to meet together for a second Bretton Woods conference on the International Monetary System. In that conference the turbulent ship of global finance could be re-anchored in solid ground – a ground which can be found only if the rich countries understand that they have to grow into new patterns of material saturation and serviceable fertility, as well as making financial room for the unfulfilled basic needs of the heavily indebted poorest countries.

Christian students in Surabaya, Indonesia, put it well in their conference about globalization. They declared that TINA, the motto that there is no alternative for our economies, is a lie; in its place they proposed a new slogan: TATA, 'There Are Thousands of Alternatives' – especially for those peoples and nations which want to act on the basis of their own true economic responsibility.[11] May their words become our words in this new millennium.

Notes

[1] For an excellent treatment of this, see A. B. Atkinson, *Poverty in Europe* (Oxford, 1998).

[2] For further information, see Stanley S. Carlson-Thies and James W. Skillen, *Welfare in America: Christian Perspectives on a Policy in Crisis* (Grand Rapids, MI, and Cambridge, 1996).

[3] Bob Goudzwaard, *Ongeprijsde schaarste, een onderzoek naar de plaats van expretiale of ongecompenseerde effecten in de theoretische economie en de leer der economische politiek* (The Hague, 1970, with an English summary).

[4] H. Johannes Witteveen, 'Economic globalization in a broader, long-term perspective: some serious concerns', in Jan Joost (ed.), *The Policy Changes of Global Financial Integration* (The Hague, 1998), 28.

[5] Cf. M. Douglas Meeks, *God the Economist: The Doctrine of God and Political Economy* (Minneapolis, 1989).

[6] Joseph A. Schumpeter, *History of Economic Analysis* (London, 1963), 417.

[7] See Bob Goudzwaard, 'Socioeconomic life: a way of confession', in Goudzwaard, *Aid for the Overdeveloped West* (Toronto, 1978), 23-33. There I discuss the hidden economic cohesion between the separate rules of the Torah. Think, for instance, about the strange rule in Deuteronomy 23: 20 which says that it is generally not permitted to claim interest for loans with the exception of loans to foreigners, whom one may compel to repay: 'On loans to a foreigner you may charge interest, but on loans to another Israelite you may not charge interest.' That is a text which appears to us to be discriminatory and just plain wrong, until we realize that Israel had to uphold its own distinctive

economy in the midst of a world in which the payment of high interest was a common practice. If every foreign banker could borrow Israelite money at an interest-level of zero without repayment, just because the law of Israel said so, all Israelite capital would have flowed immediately to the neighbouring economies. So we meet here an economic-political provision to keep the necessary capital within the Israelite borders. The system was not meant to remain utopian; it was obviously designed to work in practice and to lead the people to prosperity.

8 See Herman E. Daly and John B. Cobb, *For the Common Good: Redirecting the Economy toward Community, the Environment, and a Sustainable Future* (London, 1990), 453. The period from 1970 to 1980 marked a very slight decline of the per capita ISEW (index of sustainable economic welfare) by 0.14 per cent per year. The decline of the per capita ISEW during the 1980s by the time Daly and Cobb wrote had been 1.26 per cent per year.

9 Bob Goudzwaard and Harry de Lange, *Beyond Poverty and Affluence: Toward an Economy of Care* (Grand Rapids, MI, and Geneva, 1995), ch. 8.

10 George Goyder, *The Responsible Company* (Oxford, 1961); idem, *The Responsible Worker* (London, 1975), 130.

11 International Seminar on Alternative Economies in the Global Market System, held in Surabaya, Indonesia, 23–5 October 1996. Also cited in *Living Together in Plurality and Justice* (Social Welfare Guidance Foundation, PO Box 284, Solo, Indonesia, 1999), 30.

10

On being a Christian economist

DONALD A. HAY

My purpose in the concluding chapter of this volume is to ask a series of linked questions. The first is this. Are there problems – intellectual or ethical – for an economist, who is also a Christian, in working within the methodologies and traditions of mainstream economic analysis? The answer is that there are problems. To those outside the discipline, such an answer may seem bizarre: economics is widely presented as a technical discipline in social *science*. It seems implausible that there should be a distinctively Christian critique of economics, just as it would seem strange to ask whether the discipline of physical chemistry raises problems for Christians. The brief answer to that puzzle is that economics is a *social* science, exploring human motivations and behaviour, and relying in its normative aspects (including policy prescriptions) on a particular conception of what it is to be a human being.

The conclusion that there are problems leads naturally to our second question. How should the Christian economist respond to the problems that have been identified? Three responses can be identified in writing on the theme. The first is 'do nothing'. This may simply be an unprincipled response from Christian academic economists who are too hard-pressed with the need to get papers published and students properly taught to add to their personal intellectual agenda. But there is also a more principled view that every discipline has its own norms and traditions, and it is not appropriate to introduce extraneous matter, perhaps especially if the matter has its basis in theological ethics. A second response is to abandon mainstream economic analysis and to seek to build up an alternative paradigm based specifically in Christian principles for, and understandings of, economic life. A third response is to continue to work within the mainstream paradigm, but with

Christian critical faculties fully alert. The result will be a research agenda, and evaluative norms that transcend and on occasion displace the agenda and norms of mainstream analysis.

How we respond to the second question will evidently affect our answer to a third question. Should the policy advice that the Christian economist will address to the secular authorities be substantially different from that offered by a non-Christian economist? And how should the Christian economist deal with the difficulty that those authorities will almost certainly not share the evaluative framework that the Christian economist would wish to use.

On the values of mainstream economic analysis

In the real economic world there is an infinity of facts that we might consider. So to develop a positive economics we need an evaluative framework to identify what is of significance. These 'characterizing value judgements' are based in our presuppositions about what does and does not have value or significance. These presuppositions may just be asserted (as in the libertarian emphasis on rights), or may be deduced from some more general metaphysical world-view. They affect not only the domain of study, but also the concepts which we employ in our analysis. Hence, a 'pure' positive economics without reference to any value system is unavailable.[1]

The characterizing value judgements of contemporary economics are largely drawn from utilitarian welfare economics.[2] It was utilitarianism which gave rise to the 'rational economic man' model. Admittedly, the modern exposition of the model has been purged of cruder Benthamite notions of utility maximization, which have been replaced by the concept of maximizing our preferences, but the utilitarian 'ghost' has not been completely exorcised. Consider, for example, how frequently theoretical articles use explicit utility functions to describe preferences. The other heritage of utilitarianism has been the definition of the domain of study in economic analysis, and in particular the emphases on economic efficiency, resource allocation, growth and distribution. The objective of the economy is taken to be the maximizing of efficiency (productive and allocative) and growth, so as to be more able to satisfy the preferences of consumers.

However, the domain of economic analysis is no longer confined to economic life as usually understood – the production and distribution of goods and services. The dominant school of economic analysis within the neo-classical tradition is the 'Chicago project'. The Chicago economists (and sociologists) have made it a fundamental assumption that *all* human behaviour is driven by self-interested economic rationality; that is, people invariably choose actions which offer the greatest surplus of positive benefits over the costs of the actions. This is applied in every area of life, not just the distinctively economic. So there are, for example, flourishing research programmes in the economics of law, crime, family life, sexual relations, education, health . . . To those who object that many of these areas are surely governed by non-economic motives and values, the response is that these merely obscure the more profound workings of the forces of economic rationality. The Chicago project is by no means complete: there is always more research to be done within the framework, and models need to be made more sophisticated to capture all the nuances of self-interested behaviour in complex situations. But the commitment to the underlying paradigm is unequivocal.

The result can be some startling reinterpretations of aspects of human behaviour that we thought we understood quite differently. For example, one of the key exponents of the Chicago project, Gary Becker, has devoted his energy to the economic analysis of family life. In his Nobel Prize[3] acceptance speech, he outlined his programme as follows: 'the economic approach to the family assumes that even intimate decisions such as marriage, divorce and family size, are reached through weighing advantages and disadvantages of alternative actions . . .' So the conduct of family affairs is driven by 'incentives to invest in creating closer relations'. The concepts of moral duty and responsibilities in family life are ruled out of court a priori. Thus relationships between parents and children have nothing to do with love or altruism. The underlying motivation is implicit contracts between parents and children in which parents provide services to their children now, in the expectation that the children will support them in old age. The children are induced to keep to their side of the bargain by the expectation of an inheritance when the old folk die: indeed, this can explain why people do not consume all their wealth during their lifetime, but leave substantial sums to their children. If they have nothing to leave, then there is no incentive to the children to fulfil their part of the contract while the parents are living. In a similar vein, Richard Posner, in a book entitled *Sex and Reason*, has argued that marriage should properly be viewed as an implicit contract for sexual and other favours.[4] People get married when the economic calculus indicates that they will both gain significantly from entering into a long-term contract for sex and other goods. The partner is chosen by identifying the person who will provide maximum satisfactions for you, net of the cost to you of supplying service to him or her. Divorce occurs when the prospective gains from continuing the contract no longer outweigh the costs to you of continuing. Essentially, for Posner, there is no qualitative difference between marriage and prostitution. One is a long-term, and therefore somewhat complex, contract in which sexual relations are traded along with a bundle of other services; the other is simply a spot-market transaction in which the prostitute is paid in cash for services rendered.

The Chicago project does not stop with the family. The public-choice school analyses the political process in the same terms. Politicians, civil servants and interest groups are all driven by the pursuit of self-interest to achieve outcomes that will benefit them personally, or perhaps as a group. The older idea that public servants should seek to maximize some conception of the public good is simply a rhetorical smokescreen. At best they facilitate the bargaining process between the different interest groups, including their own interests in the process.[5]

There is no explicit normative content of the Chicago project, but the implicit assumption is that individuals are the best judges of their own interests. Since contracting between free individuals will only take place if it is to the net advantage of both parties, then whatever state of the world emerges from multiple contracting across a society is intrinsically good, and there is no need for concepts of social justice or the common good to evaluate it. Indeed, the only policy prescriptions are to avoid intervention in the contracting process between individuals, since regulation invariably reduces the possibility of net gains for some, and to avoid giving any individual a monopoly position (including political authority) as it gives them an unassailable bargaining strength. The policy prescription is therefore for minimum government (perhaps no more than a legal system to facilitate contracting and to ensure contractual performance) and for free markets.

Robert Nelson has pointed out another implication of the Chicago approach to human activity.[6] It implicitly legitimizes self-seeking behaviour in, for example, family life. In the absence of a strong moral code that suggests otherwise, it implies that if I meet someone who can provide a better 'deal' than my current marriage partner, then it is entirely 'rational' to abandon that partner and set up a new contract with the new person. Similarly, a politician schooled in the public-choice school would 'rationally' seek to maximize his own gains from decision-making, by balancing the competing lobbies clamouring for his attention in terms of the potential pay-off to him.

Despite some cogent criticisms of utilitarianism by non-economists,[7] and of rational economic man models by economists,[8] there is little doubt that this vision now dominates work by professional economists. Most econometric analysis, for example, is based on models which assume rational maximizing behaviour by economic agents. Rational expectations theory has dealt successfully with the challenge that economic agents do not have sufficient information for maximization of preferences; and competitive selection models are deemed to have excluded non-maximizing behaviour (by firms, if not by households). Even if many academic economists do not sign up to the Chicago project in all its aspects, there is at least tacit agreement that the objectives of the project are appropriate and feasible. The difficulty for many is where to draw the line between economic and non-economic aspects of life if one's personal ethic is broadly utilitarian.

The Christian critic of this methodological position might develop a critique on the basis of a biblical world-view. From that we learn that human beings are created in the image of God, with the capacity for making choices and entering into relationships; that we are stewards of the created order, to provide for our needs; that our stewardship responsibilities are to be exercised through work; and that there are explicit norms for non-economic aspects of life, like sexual relations, family life and the role of the political authorities.[9] But we also learn that human nature has been seriously affected by the Fall, so that our choices are often motivated by selfish self-interest; power and fear have entered into human relationships; stewardship of the created order has been replaced by exploitation; and our work has become toil.

It should be noted that this fallen human nature is not inconsistent with the rational economic man model, though the latter has evacuated the moral evaluation implied in the biblical concept. Indeed, this may explain why the rational economic man concept has been so enduring in economic analysis, and why the scientific research programme based on it has been so successful. However, a Christian would want to argue that the image of God was marred but not destroyed by the Fall. So the rational economic man model is incomplete: it does not encompass the human capacity to show love to a neighbour, the importance of human relationships which transcend market contracting, and the undoubted fact that for many people work is a good in itself, and not just an unfortunate necessity. Unfortunately, there is some evidence to suggest that the rational economic man model tends to legitimize selfish self-interest and thus to affect the way people behave.[10]

Moreover, the biblical material would suggest a much richer research agenda than the trinity of efficiency, growth and distribution of utilitarian welfare economics. The biblical analysis[11] suggests the following criteria for our research agenda: (i) How far do economic institutions allow human beings to exercise responsible stewardship, and encourage efficient use of resources? (ii) Is the use of natural resources characterized by care for the created order? (iii) Does the economy create opportunities for satisfying work and sufficient rest? (iv) What are the causes of poverty and are there societal mechanisms to prevent destitution? (v) Has the pursuit of wealth, for its own sake, become detrimental to other values in society, for example, family life? (vi) How effective are the authorities at promoting justice in the economic sphere? Evidently, elements of this research agenda could be addressed by non-Christian social scientists, and often are. But the overall agenda reflects a different understanding of the role of economic activity in human flourishing from that adopted by most economists.

On being a Christian and an economist

How serious is the conflict between the mainstream conception of the proper domain and content of economic analysis and the Christian understanding of economic life? As a secular interpreter of the developments in the methodology of economics, Nelson[12] argues that modern economic analysis is a secular religion. It proposes an overarching explanation of human life based on the primacy of self-seeking economic rationality and the only moral basis it allows is individual preferences. It discounts completely non-economic motivations for human action, and it sees no place for introducing any general moral principles to govern any aspect of human life, given that people can maximize their own net advantage through the contracting process. According to Nelson, it is impossible for a thinking person to operate as a mainstream economist within the dominant Chicago project and to remain a committed Christian. A Christian economist is therefore implicitly schizophrenic, or at least very muddled. Assuming that we are not satisfied with muddling along, what might we do? Three answers have been forthcoming in the literature: accept that economics is a discipline which operates with its own norms and traditions; rebuild economic analysis on Christian foundations; proceed with caution.

Accepting the autonomy of market economics

The first approach has its most surprising and distinguished advocate in John Atherton.[13] He examines three Christian responses to the market economy and finds them wanting. The first is the 'conservative' response, which he exemplifies in the work of Lord (Brian) Griffiths,[14] though he traces its origins back to the Christian political economy school of the early nineteenth century in Britain. The main justification of the market system is that it recognizes individual responsibilities and delivers on 'wealth creation', but it needs Christian values to underpin it. In particular, self-interest, the profit motive and competition need to be set within a moral and legal framework to restrain unacceptable behaviour. The 'radical' response is a complete rejection of market capitalism because of its manifest injustices, especially in the economic relations between the First and Third Worlds. According to Ulrich Duchrow,[15] the market economy is an idol writ large, and those who support it are guilty of 'heresy'. The only appropriate Christian stance is to seek to overthrow the system and replace it with some form of socialist economy. The 'liberal Protestant' response (exemplified by two social theologians, Philip Wogaman[16] in the USA and Ronald Preston[17] in the UK) also asserts the primacy of Christian values over those of the market, but understands the success of the market economy in production and growth. The relevant Christian values are derived theologically, rather than taken directly from scripture. These include the need to understand God's purposes for his world and to co-operate in those purposes, a recognition of sin, a commitment to reform linked to a high view of the state as an agent of social welfare, and social change and a preference for democratic socialism.

Atherton implicitly rejects all three responses, for two linked reasons. The first is that they all fail to do justice to the market system. The radical response and, to a lesser extent, the liberal response do not appreciate that markets have been shown to work effectively in allocating resources, and whatever its weaknesses the market system is now all that is available to us. The conservative response, in contrast, gives full support to the market mechanism, but fails to appreciate its wider social aspects. Atherton's point is that the market has its own internal logic and values which need to be understood and affirmed. The second reason for rejecting the three responses is that all three, in different ways, set Christian values above the market, where those values are derived with more or less sophistication from doctrine or scripture. Atherton explicitly and emphatically rejects the tendency to 'Christian map-making', even in such nebulous forms as the concept of the 'common good'.

How then would Atherton have us to proceed? He expounds a new approach to Christian social thought that avoids the difficulties he has identified in the three responses. He believes that our social ethics need to affirm the market as the best system we have for allocating resources. We need to recognize that the market has its own values – self-interest, efficiency, freedom in competition, individualism. We should not seek to replace these with other values, but to encourage interaction with non-market values. Moreover, we should seek to promote the 'challenges' to the market system, such as poverty, the environmental crisis, the demand for participation and the international dimensions of market relations, not with any radical objective of replacing the market, but to stimulate the market system to respond to these challenges in a positive manner. The flexibility of the market is one of its greatest advantages: it should be encouraged to adapt and change in beneficial ways. What then is the role of Christian social thought in all this? Somehow it has to enter into the interaction between the functioning and values of the market, on the one hand, and the 'challenges' to the market, on the other hand. It has to enter without a distinctively Christian agenda in mind, but with the objective of stimulating dialogue and the search for interim solutions. How this might work and what the fruits might be of such activity are not elaborated by Atherton, so it is a little difficult to see what he has in mind.

How persuasive is the case that Atherton makes, and how does it resolve the puzzle facing the Christian economist? It is certainly appropriate to ask that Christian social ethicists should make a greater effort to understand and evaluate the market system before presuming to stand in judgement on it. Atherton's affirmation of the market is perhaps a little too uncritical: most microeconomists admit that the category of 'market failure' is quite broad, and that a market economy needs quite a lot of outside 'help' if it is to function effectively. Atherton's unwillingness to permit a distinctive Christian social ethic to challenge the values of the market system is never fully justified in his work. The fact that such challenges have been inept in the past is not a strong reason for abandoning the project. Rather, his position seems to derive from a basic conviction that

> the contemporary theological task has to begin with the contemporary context . . . For beginning with the contemporary context, and pursuing a variety of objectives, themes, histories and contributions, is . . . a style of theological thought that is essentially a continual interaction between understandings of God's purposes mediated through our experiences of secular reality and through the Christian story and tradition. Explicitly Christian insights are therefore only a part of the theological task.[18]

Indeed, on the evidence of the rest of the book, Atherton is willing to accord only a minimal role to Christian insights. However, if the values of a market economy are not internally generated and autonomous (contrary to a position which Atherton shares with the Chicago project), but are substantially derived from Enlightenment or utilitarian doctrines, there is no reason why we should not attempt to introduce other values. And even if they are internally generated, then even a weak doctrine of fallen humanity should preclude Christians from accepting them uncritically. It seems unlikely that many conscientious Christian economists will feel comfortable with Atherton's approach, which would enable them to live happily with their schizophrenia.

Constructing an 'alternative' economics

The second solution to the problem is to seek to rebuild economic analysis on specifically Christian foundations. The most comprehensive attempt to do this is by economists working in the Reformed tradition, represented in the large-scale work of John Tiemstra and others,[19] which the authors tell us arose out of a major collaborative effort in the early 1980s. Their starting-point is a very careful analysis of biblical material which generates a set of principles for economic life not dissimilar to those listed above (in the section 'On the values of mainstream economic analysis'). However, their use of these principles is quite distinctive. First, they argue that economic analysis is fundamentally flawed since it is not based on Christian norms and principles. Unfortunately, much of their criticism of economic analysis, at least as a tool for analysing the reality of the secular economy, is misplaced. If the economy is based on the materialistic values of fallen human beings without God, then it seems that the rational economic man model may not be too far from a reasonable working model of economic agents. While the Christian economist's evaluation of economic life should be different, one doubts whether we need to scrap standard positive analysis and start again, as Tiemstra and his team seem to be asking. Moreover, some of their examples of flaws or deficiencies in standard neo-classical analysis seem to reflect a misreading of the literature.

The second distinctive feature of the Reformed tradition is their emphasis on institutions. The basis for this is the biblical model of human life in community, where community is expressed in institutions – family, businesses, political institutions, churches, schools, etc. Again their criticism of neo-classical analysis for failing to take institutions seriously is a bit out of date:

institutional economics became a key area of research in the late 1980s, and is now a flourishing branch of the subject. As Christians we may not like the implicit assumption of the Chicago project that family relationships, churchgoing, charitable donations and voluntary work in the community can be fully explained by economic models, but we should perhaps ponder the implications of the fact that such models seem to 'work' as explanations of actual behaviour. The Reformed critique of the Chicago project would argue that institutions like marriage have biblical norms that should completely override the self-seeking objectives and behaviour postulated by neo-classical analysis. If that is not the case empirically, as the Chicago analysis would claim, then one can try to change attitudes or even design policies to make self-seeking behaviour less attractive (though to be induced to behave 'virtuously' by an appropriate tax break is scarcely the same thing as behaving virtuously for moral reasons, and indeed any such policy could be criticized for capitulating to the Chicago view of the family!).

Finally, the Reformed approach is anxious to show that relationships in markets are more than contracting, and suggests the biblical model of covenanting as the appropriate norm. Once again, it is hard to believe that behaviour in secular markets is characterized by anything other than contracting, widely defined to include the development of long-term relationships between suppliers and customers. Such long-term relationships can be explained by normal neo-classical analysis, while accepting that the contracting model is impoverished as a form of human interaction in comparison with covenant relationships.

To sum up, it is unclear that attempts to establish an 'alternative' economic analysis are going to be successful. We may not much like what the Chicago project is telling us about human behaviour and interactions, but the truth about fallen human behaviour is unlikely, a priori, to be particularly palatable. Where Christians must differ from Chicago is in asserting that such behaviour is morally unacceptable, and that by the grace of God people can live their lives differently and virtuously. This leads us to the third option for the Christian economist: to work within the neo-classical paradigm, but to remain alert to its unacceptable normative presuppositions.

Proceeding with caution

I have noted already that biblical and theological analysis suggests a rather different understanding of human flourishing in relation to economic life from that of mainline economic analysis. The emphases on efficiency, growth and consumption of neo-classical economics are supplemented or replaced by broader concerns about responsible stewardship, care for the created order, satisfying work, alleviation of poverty, the destructive personal consequences of the pursuit of wealth, and effective action by the political authorities to promote justice in the economic sphere. The question is how the Christian economist can deploy these broader concerns in setting about his or her work. We may distinguish a subversive method and a critical method. The subversive method follows the neo-classical approach, but concentrates on some of the deeper implications of market behaviour for human flourishing. The critical method allows the biblical and theological agenda to define the research questions and to evaluate the consequences of particular aspects of economic life.

The *subversive approach* is advocated by Richardson.[20] His suggestion is that some aspects of the neo-classical research agenda ought to commend themselves to Christian economists, because their 'substance is more intrinsically interesting to Christians than other substance, and more interesting to Christians than to other spiritually minded persons or to humanists . . . the style of some economic research suits Christian temperament eminently well'.[21] Some Christian economists should get into these areas of research, seeking to emulate the rigour of the best research in the neo-classical (Chicago) tradition.[22] Indeed, he argues that there are substantial academic reputations to be won by successful analyses of these areas. His suggested areas of research are intriguing and wide-ranging. One is the extent to which an actual market system provides incentives for virtuous behaviour, penalties for bad behaviour and opportunities for losers to recover and start again. The same questions can be asked about the behaviour of whole economies in the world economy: should there, for example, be an international equivalent of domestic bankruptcy provisions for highly indebted economies, and how can the economic élites of debtor countries be prevented from walking away (to the security of their Swiss bank accounts) from the results of their improvidence or corruption? Another area is intergenerational economics, 'since markets to allow trade between the living and the yet unborn are primitive at best'.[23] The subjects to be addressed would be bequest behaviour, inheritance laws, policy towards non-renewable resources, government budget deficits and capital formation: in each case there is a question of provision for future generations. Another concern is the impact of the market forces on other communal goals, such as maintaining strong family life, providing for the poorest and treating employees fairly. Such communal goals

> are arguably inefficient (wasteful), and firms, communities, or nations that maintain them suffer discipline from unadulterated market forces. Firms with communal commitment are ripe for takeover by those with less; communities with social concern may lose businesses to communities with less; and nations may perceive foreign competition to be undermining their social policies.[24]

The implication may be that 'barriers to market forces are not only defensible, but often necessary to meet communal goals'. This agenda for research is not, of course, specifically Christian: all these subject areas are actively researched by secular economists. But the Christian subtexts are clear: rewards for good behaviour and punishment for bad, opportunities for losers to put the past behind them and start again, protection for those without a voice (the poor and the unborn), stewardship of the created order, sustaining families and other social institutions.

An excellent example of what Richardson has in mind is the work of Ben Cooper.[25] The subtext is provided by a study of the book of Ecclesiastes, which is an extended discussion on the futility of life lived without reference to God. The question addressed by the Teacher is simple: 'What does man gain from all his labour at which he toils under the sun?' (Ecclesiastes 1: 3). And the method of inquiry: 'I devoted myself to study and explore by all wisdom all that is done under heaven' (Ecclesiastes 1: 13–14). That is, the Teacher relies entirely on his own wisdom, experience and observation. The answer to the question is stark: man gains nothing, everything lacks permanence, the major cause of futility is death. Chapters 4 to 6 are specifically devoted to work, achievement and wealth. Four reasons for futility are identified: dissatisfaction arising from envy of one's neighbour

(4: 4), the isolation of the wealthy (4: 8), the fact that aspirations expand faster than our capacity to satisfy them (5: 10–11), and those with wealth are unable to enjoy it (6: 2–3). Where then is meaning to be found? Only in God (12: 13–14).

Cooper then switches to modern economic analysis. His first observation is the empirical finding that, despite a threefold to fivefold rise in income per capita in the past fifty years in the major Western economies, there was no apparent increase in average levels of satisfaction and contentment.[26] While this is fully consistent with Ecclesiastes, it is something of a puzzle for neo-classical economics. Cooper then goes on to show how it can be made consistent in a model that is entirely within the orthodox paradigm. He analyses the role of positional or status goods in a model of economic growth. Positional goods and services are those whose utility derives mainly from consuming them when our peer group does not. They might include luxury houses, status cars, foreign holidays, private education, antiques. Some are in fixed supply, for example, period houses and antiques, and as incomes grow, competition for ownership drives up their price. Consumer frustration comes from their elusiveness: despite growth in income they remain out of reach. Some disappear as consumers try to consume them: the empty and idyllic Caribbean beach becomes as crowded as any Spanish resort. Others depend on constant innovation to produce the newest status goods for which consumers are willing to pay a high price, only to find that next year they are superseded. It is this last case that Cooper and Cecilia García-Peñalosa have analysed in a formal model.[27] The finding is that, despite growth and innovation, consumer satisfaction may actually decline as more and more resources are devoted to innovating with status goods because of their intrinsic high value to consumers. Evidently, this model is highly stylized, but its message is 'subversive' in that it challenges the presumption that more goods are necessarily better, without straying outside the standard analytic framework.

The same 'subversive' quality motivated a paper in which I addressed the need for markets to have a moral framework if they are to function effectively,[28] as argued originally by Adam Smith. The context is that identified by Fred Hirsch of a depleting moral legacy in the West.[29] The solution advanced by Brian Griffiths is a revival of Christian moral values.[30] In the paper I show that, where reputation mechanisms are effective, then markets can probably function effectively without exogenous moral constraints on market behaviour. Where this condition is not fulfilled, and the evidence is that many markets do not generate good behaviour endogenously, then some solutions have to be sought – statutory regulation or self-regulation by market participants. The former is often expensive, and the latter is liable to capture: so there is much to be said for a moral code – in the words of Joan Robinson, 'Honesty is much cheaper.' The paper also addresses the question of whether markets deplete morals, and concludes that they may in circumstances where asymmetric information between supplier and customer renders the reputation mechanism less effective, and where the supplier has incentives that are linked to quantity rather than (unobservable) quality of service. An example is the National Health Service in the UK, where there is little doubt that the pre-existing values of medical vocation have been undermined in recent years by the introduction of market-type mechanisms.[31] The point about this paper is that the argument is conducted in terms of standard economic analysis without reference to theological categories – responding to what was essentially a secular discussion.

The alternative to the subversive method is the *critical method.* Here the Christian content is explicit, defining the research agenda and evaluating outcomes. One example of such work is my paper on the public joint-stock company,[32] which explores the reasons why this form of company organization has been so successful in the advanced economies. The relevant economic analyses include the role of long-term employment contracts in explaining the existence of firms, agency contracts, the need to monitor the residual claimant and the advantages of risk spreading for owners of capital. This analysis begs various ethical questions. For example, biblical principles suggest that ownership should be linked to stewardship responsibilities; in which case limited liability, indirect shareholdings (via mutual funds and other such investment vehicles) and exit rather than voice when the company is not performing well, all of which are characteristics of joint-stock companies, are ethically dubious. Against this can be set biblical injunctions to prudent behaviour (so long as this does not preclude trusting God), which would seem to support behaviour to reduce risks as part of our personal responsibility. The principle of stewardship would also appear to suggest that responsibility should rest with those who work in the company and not with some outside stakeholder. Finally, the paper questions the propriety of the takeover mechanism. If the firm is viewed fundamentally as the institution which unites those who work in it, with a key role for human capital, then those people should not be considered as the property of the capital suppliers to be sold to a bidder. The paper argues that the public trust form of company organization advocated in the UK by George Goyder[33] would solve most of these ethical questions.

In another paper,[34] I consider the allocation of resources to health care, and in particular the NHS, in the light of explicit biblical derivative social principles. These include the promotion of *shalom* ('well-being') for the patient, and not only physical health; the need for people to take responsibility for their own health with a healthy lifestyle; the supply of health care services as a merit good available on the basis of need; an obligation to help the needy, given that ill health is often a cause of poverty; and covenant rather than contract as the basis for doctor–patient relationships. The discussion suggests that the NHS scores rather well on the basis of these principles, with the exception of the second, since the incentives to care for one's own health are inevitably weakened in a system where the costs of ill health, even if self-induced, do not fall on the patient. It also suggests that market systems for the delivery of health care, including personal health insurance, are less satisfactory. They are unlikely to deliver horizontal or vertical equity, and insurance invites the moral hazard problem of people not taking sufficient care of their own health. More seriously, there are good reasons for a market system to erode good behaviour and practice by doctors, despite professional codes of conduct. Where rewards are linked to measurable indicators of 'output', such as numbers of consultations, operations and tests conducted, there will be a tendency for other aspects of the patient's *shalom* to be neglected, and for the relationship with the patient to become contractual rather than covenantal. As noted above, the introduction of quasi-market allocation mechanisms in the NHS may explain the strong sense that the quality of the service has been eroded over the last ten years.

The advantage of the critical method is that it makes the

Christian basis explicit: there is no hidden agenda. But that in turn means that work along these lines is unlikely to be read except by other Christians. Secular economists would regard it as straying too far outside the neo-classical agenda and analysis to be worthy of serious consideration.

On giving policy advice

Most economists, including academic economists, are eager to change the world as well as to understand it. On what basis then is a Christian economist to give policy advice? One possible stance is that of technician: the political authorities define their goals and the adviser presents alternative methods of achieving them on the basis of his understanding of the behaviour of the economic actors involved. Suppose, for example, that the authorities are keen to encourage single mothers to work to reduce the cost to the social security budget, not considering the impact on a small child of being separated from its mother in a crèche. An empirical labour economist would be able to estimate the degree of penalty or incentive that would induce single mothers to work, and to suggest how those incentives might be introduced so as to maximize the savings to the exchequer. While some may be comfortable with such a role, it remains a problem for some conscientious souls, especially if it involves violation of some Christian ethical principle. How then might they proceed? There are two possible stances that correspond to the subversive and critical methods just discussed.

The subversive uses the standard tools of economic analysis to evaluate fully some proposed policy changes, including all the economic impacts that can be identified. The Christian subtext is in the choice of policy area to evaluate, just as we saw that certain subject areas would naturally be more congenial for a Christian to analyse. The idea is that a Christian economist should be more motivated to undertake an objective and comprehensive analysis, and less likely to be seduced into presenting an analysis that will please the authorities or the beneficiaries of a proposed policy change. An instructive example is given by Earl Grinols,[35] who is Professor of Economics at the University of Illinois. In 1990, he was disturbed to read a newspaper announcement of a plan to open an off-track betting parlour for his town. He was even more surprised that the supporters of the project believed that it would create 125 jobs in the town. As a Christian he was opposed to gambling, and decided to devote some of his professional time to making estimates of the economic gains and losses from casino operations in the USA. Contrary to the advocates of gambling, he was able to show that the measurable social costs of gambling are indeed substantial and that, on standard economic evaluations, tough regulation would be appropriate. First, the social costs of gambling exceed the social benefits (profits to the casino owners, wages and taxes) by at least a factor of two. The main social costs arise from the phenomenon of problem gamblers: if a casino is opened in an area, between one and two people out of every 100 in the locality will become pathological gamblers suffering from symptoms of addiction, and another two or three will become problem gamblers with less serious addictive behaviour. Studies in Wisconsin showed that each one of these people cost society $10,000 per annum in social support of one kind and another. That figure does not include the cost of crimes committed by problem gamblers, such as embezzlement, credit card fraud and false insurance claims, for which there is insufficient detailed evidence. Nor does it include the lost productivity of gambling activity. Most gamblers describe their gambling activity in non-recreational terms – they are in it to make money (they hope). So time spent gambling represents output lost to society. Grinols also found persuasive evidence to suggest that the supposed benefits of a casino in terms of economic development and employment did not exist. In Illinois he found that 75 per cent of casino revenue came from residents who live within a 35-mile radius of the casino, and another 10–20 per cent from those living within a 50-mile radius. The effect on the local economy is that, for every $1,000 dollars of casino revenue, local spending within a 10-mile radius falls by at least $460. The profit rates on revenue from casinos are huge: Grinols quotes the case of one casino near Chicago where profits were 47 per cent of revenues. Furthermore, those profits are usually taken out of the local economy rather than reinvested.

The critical approach to policy makes the Christian values and agenda explicit. Evidently, any policy proposals based on such values will not easily be commended to those who do not accept a Christian world-view and ethic. One possible response is to proceed on the basis of those values, but without stating a specifically Christian rationale. This is, for example, the approach taken by the Relationships Foundation, which grew out of the Jubilee Centre at Cambridge. In their book, *The R Factor*, Michael Schluter and David Lee spell out a number of desirable characteristics of social and economic arrangements based on giving the quality of human relationships priority over economic efficiency and growth.[36] These characteristics are based on a set of assumptions about human well-being that are not flagged up as specifically Christian, but are certainly compatible with Christian values. This is closer to a natural-law approach: the assumption is that thoughtful people of other religious persuasions, or of no faith at all, will find the characteristics persuasive. I will not consider this approach further here, not because I necessarily regard it as invalid, but because, if it is skilfully undertaken, any Christian content is effectively suppressed. So I focus on procedures where a Christian ethic is made explicit.

The main question to be addressed is whether Christian ethics for economic life can be developed with sufficient precision to enable us to say anything distinctive about policy issues. Some have doubted this,[37] and, looking at the variety of prescriptions that have come from Christians on various economic issues, there seems to be at least some basis for doubt. I proceed by means of an example. The welfare state has been an important theme in the writings of Ronald Preston,[38] probably the most significant social theologian writing about economic issues in the UK in the last twenty-five years.[39] Preston begins with three powerfully stated theological themes which he claims characterize the Christian basis for economic and social life: that human life is irreducibly social and expressed as much in our interdependence as in our individuality, that there is an absolute duty to protect and provide for the poor and the disadvantaged, and that human affairs are marred by sin and social disintegration. Refining these concepts somewhat, Preston arrives at three principles: citizenship, participation and equality, and justice for the poor. On this basis he establishes a case for a welfare system, and is able to rule out one model which sees the state as simply a safety net in cases where private provision (individual, family or community-based) fails. But one could easily dismiss all this as 'motherhood and apple pie': most thoughtful people would agree without any appeal to theological ethics. The hard questions are about how to implement a welfare system in which the state is either a primary provider of social security or a primary funder. Should the focus be on equality of material outcomes or on equality of opportunity? Should there be a distinction between the 'deserving' and the 'undeserving' poor? If the principles of citizenship and participation hold, then presumably the system should be directed at relative rather than absolute poverty, but how should the poverty line be set? How exactly should a balance be achieved between state provision of pensions and provision by the individual, family or community? How decentralized should the system be, and to what extent should the poor be involved in deciding the distribution of benefits? How important is it to avoid disincentives to work, and should unemployment benefits be linked to a requirement to take work if it is offered? Finally, should benefits be universal rights (as Beveridge argued at the beginning of the welfare state in Britain), or should they be targeted on those who need assistance most acutely? The point is that, on the general principles advanced by Preston, few, if any, of these specific questions can be answered. Economic analysis does not find them easy either, but at least the standard efficiency/equity analysis gives a framework within which they can be sensibly addressed.

The problem arises because the principles advanced by Preston are too ill-defined. Citizenship obviously involves rights and responsibilities. But what rights and what responsibilities? Participation could be in production, consumption or decision-taking. Are all three required? Equality has several dimensions: we have already noted equality of opportunity and equality of outcomes. Perhaps we should add equality of power. We should note that for Preston there is no particular problem here, because of the method of 'doing' social ethics that he favours. This is the misleadingly entitled 'middle axioms' method.[40] In this method the social theologian enters into dialogue with experts in the field seeking to establish more detailed principles and policies, but without any explicit Christian agenda. At best, the theologian contributes insights from his or her Christian world-view. The danger is that the Christian element in the final report on the dialogue may turn out to be minimal, crowded out by the contributions of the experts.[41] The alternative to Preston's method is to make the Christian insights more precise. Nigel Biggar and I show, for example, that the biblical material on 'social security systems' in ancient Israel and in the New Testament church can provide some useful additional precepts.[42] These include the principle that the first defence against poverty is productive work, that decision-making in welfare systems should be devolved and the recipients should have a voice, and that selectivity is acceptable so long as it can be applied without demeaning the claimant. But even with these additional principles, there are still plenty of questions left unresolved, and it is unclear where to go next to resolve them.[43] The problem is even worse in some other areas of economic policy. The question of welfare systems can appeal to a relatively rich vein in the biblical texts, with a variety of relevant passages. On other critical questions there is virtually nothing (for example, the scope and conduct of monetary policy in an advanced economy, or whether Britain should enter European Monetary Union). So one is left to construct arguments from very general biblical principles for economic life. Unfortunately, there is virtually no tradition of constructing such arguments – largely, one suspects, because social theologians have not thought that it is an appropriate way to proceed in the circumstances. So there is no literature to give examples of 'good practice'. There remains a lot of work to be done here, if one is convinced that this is an appropriate way of tackling economic issues from a Christian perspective.

On where we stand

The chapter began by posing the question whether the values and methods of mainstream economic analysis are in conflict with Christian understandings of the values and purposes of economic life. My conclusion is that they are. The rational economic man model, with its intellectual roots in utilitarianism, is too narrow a foundation for normative analysis. Its disturbing descriptive realism can be traced to the radical self-centredness of fallen humanity, but there is more, much more, to being fully human in our economic activity. The Christian economist should seek to address a much wider set of values, and a correspondingly broader agenda for research, based on stewardship, care for the created order, good work and sufficient rest, and concern for the poor and disadvantaged. Moreover, the Christian economist will not accept the attempts to extend the logic of rational economic man to areas of human life that are not intrinsically to do with economics – sexual relations, the family and political life. Models of social interaction that assume that relationships are best modelled as mutually beneficial trades of services may (sadly) be descriptively accurate, but can never supply an appropriate normative framework.

How can the economist who is also a Christian live with the implicit tension between the intellectual norms of his or her discipline and the values that arise from a Christian world-view? One solution is to accept the tension and live a divided life: indeed, that can be a principled decision, accepting that the market has its own values, and not presuming to impose a Christian moral map on a secular discipline. The other extreme solution is to abandon standard economic analysis, and to rebuild the discipline on Christian values. My preferred solution is to use economic analysis with caution, accepting that it may be an adequate description of economic behaviour in a market economy, but rejecting its normative claims. That cautious use may be subversive, showing some of the unexpected consequences of behaviour motivated by human sinfulness in the context of a market economy, but without introducing a specifically Christian agenda. But it may also be critical, evaluating economic activity in the light of overt Christian values, and pinpointing the failures of the market economy.

The same subversive and critical approaches can be used in framing policy. The former, as the study of gambling in the USA showed, can identify effects that should give even the most committed advocate of the 'free market' food for thought. The latter has explicit Christian values much in evidence, and makes them part of the policy analysis. But attempts to implement this programme are not always fruitful: Christian ethics for economic life are often too imprecise to generate clear policy criteria. What remains unclear is whether this is a problem that can be addressed by more careful development of our ethical thinking, or whether greater precision must always elude us.

Notes

[1] This point is persuasively argued in D. M. Hausman and M. McPherson, *Economics and Moral Philosophy* (Cambridge, 1996).

[2] See my *Economics Today: A Christian Critique* (Leicester and Grand Rapids, 1989), chap. 3, for a fuller exposition of the role of utilitarian welfare economics in economic analysis.

[3] Gary Becker, 'Nobel lecture: the economic way of looking at behaviour', *Journal of Political Economy*, 101/3 (1993), 402. The fact that Becker was awarded the Nobel Prize for economics should alert us to the fact that the Chicago project is no longer regarded as extreme within the economics mainstream.

[4] Richard A. Posner, *Sex and Reason* (Cambridge, MA, 1992).

[5] Dennis C. Mueller, *Public Choice*, 2nd edn (Cambridge, 1992).

[6] Robert H. Nelson, 'Economic religion versus Christian values', paper presented at conference of the American Association of Christian Economists, 5–6 January 1998 in Chicago, IL. See also his *Reaching for Heaven on Earth: The Theological Meaning of Economics* (Savage, MD, 1991). Nelson is an economist.

[7] Bernard Williams, 'A critique of utilitarianism', in Amartya K. Sen and Bernard Williams, *Utilitarianism and Beyond* (Cambridge, 1984).

[8] Amartya K. Sen, 'Rational fools: a critique of the behavioural foundations of economic theory', *Philosophy and Public Affairs*, 6 (1976–7), 317–44.

[9] A very similar list emerges from the different ethical method adopted by Roman Catholic moral theologians: see, for example, *Centesimus Annus* (1991), a papal encyclical which provides an excellent summary of Catholic teaching on these matters. Interestingly, the encyclical also includes a fairly extensive commentary on relevant biblical material, though this is introduced to illustrate and complement moral principles derived from a more theological approach.

[10] R. H. Franks, T. Gilovich and D. Regan, 'Does studying economics inhibit cooperation?', *Journal of Economic Perspectives*, 7/2 (1993), 159–71.

[11] See my *Economics Today*, chs. 1 and 2, for an interpretation of the relevant biblical material.

[12] Nelson, *Reaching for Heaven*.

[13] John Atherton, *Christianity and the Market: Christian Social Thought for our Times* (London, 1992).

[14] Brian Griffiths, *Morality and the Market Place* (London, 1980); idem, *The Creation of Wealth* (London, 1984).

[15] Ulrich Duchrow, *Global Economy: A Confessional Issue for the Churches?* (Geneva, 1987). Duchrow is Professor of Theology at Heidelberg University and a WCC consultant. According to Atherton, Duchrow's

radical stance grew out of his first-hand experience of poverty during time spent in Brazil.

16 J. Philip Wogaman, *Christians and the Great Economic Debate* (London, 1977).

17 Ronald Preston, *Religion and the Persistence of Capitalism* (London, 1979); idem, *Church and Society in the late Twentieth Century* (London, 1983); idem, *Religion and the Ambiguities of Capitalism* (London, 1991).

18 Atherton, *Christianity and the Market*, 22.

19 J. P. Tiemstra, *Reforming Economics: Calvinist Studies on Methods and Institutions* (Lewiston, NY, 1990).

20 J. D. Richardson, 'Frontiers in economics and Christian scholarship', *Christian Scholars Review,* 17 (1988), 381–405, repr. in *Bulletin of the Association of Christian Economists,* 23 (1994), 16–33. Page references which follow are to the reprint.

21 Richardson, 'Frontiers', 22.

22 Richardson's first expressed concern is that Christian economists should be outstanding professionals in their field, both in the quality of their published work and their contribution as academic leaders and teachers, and he laments the fact that there are no professing Christians among the world's leading economists.

23 Ibid., 23.

24 Ibid.

25 B. Cooper, 'Futile growth and the economics of Ecclesiastes', *Journal of the Association of Christian Economists*, 25 (1998), 1–13.

26 A. Oswald, 'Happiness and economic performance', *Economic Journal,* 107 (1997), 1815–31.

27 Ben Cooper and Cecilia García-Peñalosa, *Status Effects and Negative Utility Growth* (Nuffield College, Oxford, Discussion Paper, 150; Oxford, 1998).

28 Donald A. Hay, 'Do markets need a moral framework?', in A. Montefiore and D. Vines (eds.), *Integrity in the Private and Public Domain* (London, 1999).

29 F. Hirsch, *The Social Limits to Growth* (London, 1977).

30 Griffiths, *Morality and Market Place* and *Creation of Wealth.*

31 There is here, I surmise, a fruitful area for further research. Much has been written about the role of the Protestant ethic in the emergence of capitalism in the West. One question is whether capitalism can flourish without that ethic, or whether it will just have very different characteristics.

32 Donald A. Hay, 'The public joint-stock company: blessing or curse?', *Journal of the Association of Christian Economists,* 8 (1989), 19–47.

33 George Goyder, *The Just Enterprise* (London, 1987).

34 Donald A. Hay, 'Christian perspectives on the economics of the

National Health Service', *Journal of the Association of Christian Economists,* 25 (1998), 14–30.

[35] Earl L. Grinols, 'Gambling economics: a primer', *Bulletin of the Association of Christian Economists,* 28 (1996), 25–32.

[36] Michael Schluter and David J. Lee, *The R Factor* (London, 1993).

[37] P. S. Williams, 'Hermeneutics for economists: issues in interpretation', *Journal of the Association of Christian Economists,* 22 (1996), 13–37, see esp. pp. 30–1.

[38] Preston, *Persistence of Capitalism*; idem, *Church and Society*; idem, *Ambiguities of Capitalism* (see n. 17).

[39] The discussion which follows is based on the analysis of Preston's writings in N. Biggar and D. A. Hay, 'The Bible, Christian ethics and the provision of social security', *Studies in Christian Ethics,* 7 (1994), 43–64.

[40] Misleading because it gives an impression of a logical process, which it certainly is not.

[41] Preston appears not to be aware that the experts are seldom disinterested technicians without their own system of values that they bring to the discussion. As already noted, secular economists subscribe, consciously or unconsciously, to the set of values which are implicit in modern economic analysis.

[42] Biggar and Hay, 'The Bible, Christian ethics'.

[43] Roman Catholics have the undoubted advantage of a much better developed system of ethical thought, and can generally make rather more progress on detailed ethical issues than can Protestants. But the principles expounded in the papal encyclicals that deal with economic matters, for example, *Centesimus Annus* (1991), are still at a very high level of generality, though elegantly stated and argued.

Index